DUNDEE

but not as we know it!

A quirky new guide to the City of Discovery

SUSAN McMULLAN

BLACK & WHITE PUBLISHING

First published 2015
by Black & White Publishing Ltd
29 Ocean Drive, Edinburgh EH6 6JL

1 3 5 7 9 10 8 6 4 2   15 16 17 18

ISBN: 978 1 84502 960 9

ALBA | CHRUTHACHAIL

A CIP catalogue record for this book is available from the British Library.
Typeset by Creative Link, North Berwick
Printed and bound in Poland by www.hussarbooks.pl

For my fabulous friend, Gill Ballie – Dundee's very own ray of sunshine.

Contents

Introduction

Think you know Dundee? Think again!

Dundee is one of Scotland's most inspired cities. It is known worldwide as the City of Discovery thanks to its history of scientific breakthroughs, Captain Scott's famous Antarctic exploration ship and of course, its jute, jam and journalism – all of which have paved the way for the melting pot of culture, innovation and learning that exists today.

As Scotland's fourth largest city, Dundee is also officially Scotland's sunniest city and enjoys a prominent position on the Tay Estuary on the East coast of Scotland.

The first record of a settlement known as Dundee was made in 1054. The town became a Royal Burgh in 1191 thanks to King William I of Scotland but with no official documents confirming this status, King Robert the Bruce issued a new Charter in 1327. Dundee received its Royal Charter as a city in 1889.

The origin of the name 'Dundee' has many claims but it is thought to be of Gaelic descent and means 'Hill of God' or 'Hill of Tay'.

Originally a sea-faring and market town, Dundee has experienced a number of turbulent periods throughout history, including its occupation by the English in 1291 as part of the Scottish Wars of Independence.

Linen formed the basis of the growth of the textiles industry in Dundee. From the seventeenth century through to the mid-nineteenth century, linen and then flax were the town's mainstays. Jute was also important to the extent that in the 1860s, Dundee was known as 'Juteopolis' in recognition of its global significance in the jute industry. During that time, Dundee employed more than 50,000 people in over 100 mills across the city. In fact, jute remained Dundee's single largest employer until as recently as 1966 when changing demands led to diversification.

The rise of the jute trade brought with it the increased expansion of important supporting industries, such as whaling, fishing and shipbuilding – all of which shaped the development of the city. At the same time, Dundee became famous for smaller industries, notably publishing and the production of marmalade.

Fast-forward to the twenty-first century and Dundee is now better known for its internationally recognised life sciences sector and for its pioneering developments in the gaming industry. It also plays a leading role in education, medicine, art, sport, music and politics and is the UK's first Unesco City of Design – making it one of Scotland's key cities.

In fact, as the host of the new Victoria and Albert Museum on the revitalised waterfront, Dundee once again finds itself at the centre of burgeoning reinvention and revolutionary change – its spirit strongly rooted in its rich heritage of success and innovation.

Of course, in a city that has experienced so much transformation over the years, it is perhaps not surprising that within Dundee, there lurks a rich tapestry of overlooked gems and forgotten moments from days gone by – all just waiting to be discovered. And what better place to discover, than in the city famous for its discoveries?

Dundee, But Not As We Know It! takes the reader on an alternative journey through the city and encourages people to open their eyes to the history that is on their doorstep and under their feet. It aims to inspire visitors and locals alike to discover some of Dundee's hidden treasures. There's more to Dundee than meets the eye.

Central

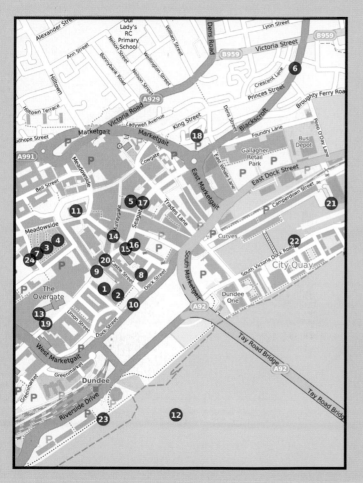

1. The Second Largest Emerald Ever Discovered
2. The Finest Concert Organ in Scotland
3. The Howff
4. The Nine Incorporated Trades
5. Dundee's Last Witch (? – 1669)
6. Jack the Ripper in Dundee
7. James Chalmers: Inventor of the Adhesive Postage Stamp
8. Water, Water Everywhere!
9. Dundee's Trams
10. The Royal Arch
11. The Tay Whale
12. The *Mars* Training Ship
13. Mary Slessor: A Dundee Missionary Abroad
14. Dundee's Dragon
15. William Wallace in the City of Discovery
16. The Castle of Dundee
17. The Town House
18. Gates and Ports
19. The Mercat Cross and The Tron
20. Gardyne's Land
21. The Submarine Memorial
22. Dundee's Other Ship
23. World Record Seaplane Flight
24. Dundee's Time Capsule

1. The Second Largest Emerald Ever Discovered

If ever there was a jewel in the crown, this is it! On 10 July 1914, King George V and Queen Mary visited Dundee. The purpose of their trip was to lay the foundation stone of the Caird Hall, the city's grand new concert and events venue.

During their visit, the Royal couple took part in what was then a unique ceremony. At Ashton Works in the Hawkhill area of Dundee, they each pressed electronic buttons under the watchful eye of benefactor and jute baron Sir James Key Caird (1837–1916), who gifted the venue to the city. The buttons triggered the lowering of the foundation stone into place in the Greenmarket region of the city, which was more than a mile away. The stone can still be seen today incorporated into the wall at the back of the Caird Hall on Shore Terrace.

King George pressed an emerald button and Queen Mary pressed a jade button. Both of the buttons were then presented to Their Majesties as a memento of the occasion. Queen Mary accepted the jade stone but the King handed the emerald back to Sir James Caird, with the instruction that it should remain in the hands of the city for its benefit.

The emerald was then incorporated into the Lord Provost's Chain of Office and it remains there to this day.

Emeralds, as with other gems, come in a variety of different sizes and forms. Those used in jewellery are typically very clear and although not often 'perfect', they do have brilliance similar to rubies and sapphires. The stone incorporated into the Chain of Office is a grand example of a cloudy emerald. These are very rarely used to form gemstones and remarkably, the Dundee emerald is known to be the second-largest emerald ever discovered.

It is so rare in fact, that it is almost impossible to put

a realistic value on the stone, making it one of Dundee's true hidden gems.

Despite significant research, the history of the stone remains unknown and there is no official documentation to confirm where it was mined, where it was purchased or how much was paid for it.

All that does exist is hearsay that the stone may have been found in Brazil but nothing to verify this claim has ever been uncovered. Dundee's hidden treasure may have a hidden history all of its own . . . .

Guided tours of the City Chambers to see the Chain of Office and other civic regalia can be arranged, subject to availability.

2. The Finest Concert Organ in Scotland

Unbeknownst to many, the Caird Hall is home to one of Dundee's cultural jewels – the 3-manual and pedal organ. Hailed as the finest concert organ in Scotland, it is also one of the leading concert hall organs in the United Kingdom.

The organ was designed by the renowned organist of St George's Church in Edinburgh, Alfred Hollins (1865–1942), who was blind. Hollins was born in Yorkshire, and was blind from birth. It is said that he was pitch perfect at a very young age and that his command of the piano in early childhood proved his genius. He was educated by, and worked for, some of the musical greats of his time and performed all over the world. He became a composer and teacher and is regarded as one of the most charismatic organists of the last 150 years.

The Caird Hall organ was built by Harrison & Harrison of Durham in 1922 and was installed in 1923. It has fifty speaking stops, which determine the different pitches and tones of the organ. The main part of the organ case is made of wood and all the pipes that are visible are speaking pipes. In the centre of the wooden case, in the most prominent position in the hall, is a depiction of the Coat of Arms of Dundee. It shows a pot of three lilies that represent St Mary, Dundee's Patron Saint, on a blue shield with a green wyvern on either side.

The Caird Hall itself is one of Dundee's best-loved buildings. It was gifted to the city by local jute baron and philanthropist, Sir James Key Caird (1837–1916) and was constructed between 1914 and 1922. Mindful of the money he had made in his mill, Sir James Caird donated £100,000 towards the construction of a City Hall and Council Chambers. Sir James Caird's gift of the Caird Hall to Dundee was the highlight of an incredible record of public benevolence that extended over a period of thirty years.

In 1991, the Caird Hall organ underwent a complete

restoration, carried out by the original builders. As part of this, the pitch was sharpened to make the organ playable with orchestras and instrumentalists.

Today, the charitable organisation the 'Friends of the Caird Hall Organ' works to promote and support the organ to give as many people as possible the opportunity to hear it being played. The charity aims to secure the long-term future of the organ as part of Dundee's cultural heritage. It holds regular recitals and events throughout the year for all to enjoy and facilitates local educational programmes.

Guided tours of the Caird Hall are provided for members of the public on request, subject to availability. Offering the chance to see the organ up close, this is an opportunity not to be missed.

3. The Howff

The Howff is an ancient burial ground located in the heart of Dundee's city centre. It has existed since around 1564 and sits on land that was originally the orchard or gardens of the Franciscan Monastery.

At this time, the main place of burial in Dundee was attached to St Mary's Church but it had become contaminated and unfit for use. An effective solution came when, during a visit to Dundee on 11 September 1564, Mary, Queen of Scots granted the citizens of Dundee the right to use the Monastery's land as a cemetery.

The name Howff comes from an old Scots word meaning 'meeting place'. The Bakers Trade of Dundee met there in 1576, and in 1581, an agreement was signed in the Howff which united the Nine Trades of Dundee into one organisation. The Nine Incorporated Trades, which promoted fair trade within the city and consisted of representatives from Dundee's key trades, met at The Convener's Stone – a central marker in the cemetery. In order to do so, they paid the town council an annual rent of £5 12s 0d. The convention held its meetings there until 1776 when it moved to a new, purpose-built Trades Hall in the High Street, which has since been demolished.

Up until 1821, there were no regulations as to the removal or modernisation of tombstones in the Howff and many were taken down and used in other monuments or for building purposes. In 1823, the Howff underwent extensive renovations and by 1835, a new cemetery, 220 yards to the north, was built by the town and called the New Howff. Despite this, by 1857 a further 14,250 people had been buried in the original Howff and conditions had become so bad that an application was lodged for its closure. Against much public protest, the Howff was closed to general burials in November 1860. The last person to

be buried there was George Duncan, MP, in 1878. In total, some 80,000 burials took place in the Howff and New Howff combined.

The memorials of many leading citizens can be found in the Howff, adding to the site's historical significance. Look out for the gravestone of James Chalmers (1782–1853), who is said to have invented the adhesive postage stamp, and John Glas, (1695–1773), a clergyman and founder of the Glasite movement. Of special interest also is Doctor David Kinloch (1559–1617), mediciner to James VI and at one time imprisoned by the Spanish Inquisition. It is recorded that he was freed on curing James VI of a serious illness. The grave that is thought to be the oldest in the cemetery is dated 4 December 1577 and belongs to a Mr Thomas Muir.

Today, locals still use the Howff as a meeting place but in a more informal manner and people can often be seen there relaxing and soaking up the sun during the summer months.

4. The Nine Incorporated Trades

The Nine Incorporated Trades was formed in Dundee in 1581 and consisted of, in order of importance: the Baxters (bakers), the Cordiners (shoemakers), the Skinners (glovemakers), the Tailors, the Bonnetmakers, the Fleshers (butchers), the Hammermen (metal workers), the Websters (weavers) and the Litsters (dyers who amalgamated with the waulkers or fullers of cloth).

The original purpose of Dundee's Nine Trades, whose motto is 'Nine in One', was to ensure that members received a reasonable price for their services, to promote fair trade and to discourage non-members from undercutting the price of their goods. By being part of the Incorporation, members enjoyed influential political powers and many took an active interest in the welfare of Dundee.

The Nine Trades held their meetings at various locations throughout Dundee until Mary, Queen of Scots gifted the citizens of Dundee the right to use the orchard of the Franciscan Monastery as a cemetery. This cemetery became known as the 'Howff' meaning 'meeting place' and the Nine Trades met there until 1776 when they were able to open their new Trades Hall. This purpose-built meeting place was located at the top of the Murraygate and consisted of shops on the ground level and meeting places on the upper levels. At the opening ceremony, the Nine Trades gathered at the Howff and marched to their new hall.

A similar journey was repeated in 1976 to commemorate the 200th anniversary of the opening of St Andrews Church, which itself was funded by the Nine Trades. Today, the Trades meet at this church, originally known as the Trades' Kirk, every year on the Sunday nearest to St Andrews Day, for a service known as 'the Kirkin' of the Trades'. The original purpose of this service was to allow the new Deacons to introduce themselves to their trades.

The Trades Hall, however, was under-used. In 1864, the Hall was sold and in 1876 it was demolished as part of plans to improve the city.

The records of the Nine Trades are held in the Lockit Books, so-called because they have hasps with a lock. The Books detail the names of everyone who has ever been admitted as a Master to any of the Trades and they note the rules, acts and statutes of each craft.

Many of the Trades enjoyed their own traditions. For example, until the Reformation, Dundee's Cordiners held a procession in honour of their Patron Saint, Crispin. After the Reformation, the parade became known as King Crispin's and the festival of St Crispin was celebrated by Cordiners throughout Europe. Visit the McManus Art Gallery and Museum to view the 33 feet-long painting that depicts one of Dundee's King Crispin's Parades. The painting was originally hung around the walls of the Cordiners' room in the Trades Hall and was painted in 1778 by Alexander Methven, who died before it was finished.

Local artist Henry Harwood completed the work in 1825.

Alongside the Nine Trades were the building trades, known as the Three United Trades of Dundee, namely the Masons, Wrights (cabinetmakers) and Slaters. They were granted their Charter to Incorporate in 1741 but had existed for hundreds of years before then. The Three United Trades had no official say in the affairs of the town, however when a new building was created or a new public body was set up, they were usually involved and donated funds towards local charities.

In fact, the Nine Trades and The Three Trades worked together with the Kirk Session to build St Andrew's Church in 1776.

Each Trade enjoyed a monopoly over its particular craft from medieval times until 1846, when the Trades lost their privileges and their aims changed to meet the social and economic circumstances of the day.

Today, the Nine Incorporated Trades continues to work as a charitable organisation, helping to promote education in the city.

5. Dundee's Last Witch (? –1669)

Grissell Jaffray was the last person to be executed in Dundee for the crime of witchcraft and cavorting with the devil.

An order for her trial was issued by the Privy Council and she was found guilty. She was convicted of being in league with the devil and sentenced to death. In 1669, Jaffray was strangled, as was common practice, before being burnt at the stake.

There are no details to confirm exactly what crimes Jaffray was found guilty of or what she is alleged to have done and much of her story remains unknown.

During the sixteenth and seventeenth centuries, it was not unusual for women to be accused of witchcraft for behaviour such as gossiping or acting out of jealousy. At a time of deep religious unrest and general mistrust, periodic witch-hunts, mainly targeting women who performed 'suspicious' acts such as mixing herbs or chanting verse, led to witch trials. The

Scottish Witchcraft Act of 1563 made witchcraft and consorting with witches, devils and spirits, an offence which was punishable by death.

What is known, however, is that Jaffray was a respectable citizen who was married to a city burgess. She was burned in the playfield or archery butts of Dundee beyond Westport and today a mosaic that depicts her punishment can be seen in Peter Street in the Seagate.

Not surprisingly, there are many stories that have come to be associated with Dundee's last witch. One such story tells of how Grissell Jaffray's son brought his ship into Dundee on the day of his mother's execution and when he was told that the smoke rising above the city was that of his mother's burning body, he turned and sailed away – never to return to Dundee.

Other stories claim that her grave can be seen in the Howff cemetery. The Convener's Stone in the graveyard is reputed to be the marker for Grissell Jaffray. It can be easily identified by the collection of coins that appear on top of the stone. Nobody knows why or when the tradition of placing coins on top of this pillar came to be, or how someone accused of witchcraft could be buried in consecrated ground. Some say that this 'witches' stone' was in fact one of the largest stones in the graveyard before those in power opted to eradicate Jaffray's name from history.

Of course, many refute this story on the basis that there would be nothing left to bury after the body of a witch had been burnt. However, whatever is true, it is clear that Grissell Jaffray left a lasting impression on a city that viewed her with such fear.

6. Jack the Ripper in Dundee

The last public execution by hanging in Dundee took place on 24 April 1889. William Henry Bury (1859–1889) faced his sentence for murdering his wife by strangling and stabbing her and then keeping her body in a trunk for several days before confessing to the crime.

Bury was a sawdust merchant and came to Dundee in search of work. He was from the Whitechapel area of London – the notorious hunting ground of the grisly killer, Jack the Ripper. Many people believed that Bury might have actually been Jack the Ripper, as the infamous murders stopped when Bury was executed. He was first named publicly as a possible Ripper suspect by the *New York Times*.

Bury and his wife Ellen, a former prostitute, arrived in Dundee in 1889. They lived at 43 Union Street and then at 113 Princes Street, where Bury murdered Ellen and for several days kept her body in the trunk that

they had used to carry their luggage from London. He even played cards with friends on top of the trunk, with his wife hidden inside, before handing himself in to the police and proclaiming that he was Jack the Ripper.

It is said that before his confession, Bury had several discussions with a male friend about Jack the Ripper, raising suspicions that Bury himself could well have been the ill-famed murderer.

Added to these suspicions was the evidence that Ellen Bury's murder followed a similar pathology to the Jack the Ripper murders. The Ripper was known to have murdered at least five women, all of them prostitutes. Bury killed a former prostitute, albeit his wife and Ellen lost her life in a similar, though not identical, way to the Ripper victims – strangulation followed by mutilation.

As well as this, according to reports from the *Dundee Courier* on Tuesday 12 February 1889, there was an inscription in the back stairwell to Bury's premises that read, 'Jack Ripper is in this seller [sic]'

and another that said, 'Jack Ripper is at the back of the door'. The graffiti suggested that possibly Bury himself or his neighbours thought that he was Jack the Ripper. There are of course, lots of different opinions about the inscription – it could have simply been drawn by children and it could even have been there long before Bury lived in the building.

Bury also broadly matched the description of the Ripper: they were both stocky, dark-haired and wore long, black coats and peaked caps.

However, detectives at the time were divided in their opinions about Bury. Many believed that his Ripper confession was false and that the reason he killed his wife was to claim her money. As a result, they officially concluded that the Dundee murder was an isolated incident and was not associated with the Ripper killings at all.

Although Bury never actually confessed to the Ripper murders, his hangman, James Berry, was convinced that Bury was Jack the Ripper. One of the detectives sent from London to investigate the murder was said to have agreed with the hangman, proclaiming that he was satisfied Berry had hanged Jack the Ripper and that from that moment on there would be no more Whitechapel crimes. No records of another Ripper murder were recorded after Ellen Bury's death.

Bury's hanging was the last time that the black flag was hoisted above the court building in Dundee to announce the death sentence had been carried out and 5,000 people came to see the flag raised.

The case against Bury as Jack the Ripper clearly cannot be proved beyond reasonable doubt but neither, it seems, can it be entirely disproved. To this day, there is more evidence against Bury than any other known suspect.

The mystery continues.

7. James Chalmers: Inventor of the Adhesive Postage Stamp

James Chalmers (1782–1853), was a Dundonian bookseller, printer and newspaper publisher.

It is also claimed that he was the inventor of the pre-paid adhesive postage stamp. A fiery debate encircles this claim and Chalmers' son, Patrick Chalmers (1819–1891), campaigned throughout his life to have his father recognised for his invention – an invention that formed the basis of our present day mailing system.

From the mid-1820s James Chalmers campaigned for improvements to the speed of the postal service between Edinburgh and London. He eventually succeeded and the time it took for mail to be delivered was reduced in each direction by one full day.

During this period, the postal service was disorganised and charges varied according to the distance the mail had to travel. In fact, there was no way of showing on the mail that postage had been paid. The Penny Post was therefore introduced in 1840, providing a single rate of postage and in the same year the Penny Black, the world's first adhesive postage stamp, was invented.

Many argue that the Penny Post was created by James Chalmers a year before Englishman Sir Rowland Hill was officially named as the inventor. The story goes that Rowland Hill also campaigned for Post Office reform and an increase in the speed of delivery. His supporters believe it was Hill who argued that there should be a standard rate for sending letters in Britain, regardless of distance and that stamps should be introduced as payment. The Penny Black is said to have been a direct result of his work, paving the way for the passage of the Penny Postage Bill. Rowland Hill was therefore made superintendent of the system, secretary to the Post Office and later knighted.

This outraged Chalmers and one of his former

employees anonymously published a letter in the *Dundee Courier* that claimed that James Chalmers had created a plan before 1837 to reform the postal service and to introduce the pre-paid adhesive postage stamp. More letters supporting this claim were published and were sent to Chalmers' son who used the evidence to conclude that his father invented the adhesive postage stamp in 1834.

The newspaper also claimed that Chalmers told Robert Wallace, MP for Greenock, about his ideas and that in 1839 when the Penny Postage Bill was passed, Wallace encouraged the House of Commons to adopt the adhesive postage stamp.

Chalmers entered a public competition to come up with a plan to make the new postage system work. His ideas around the size and shapes of the stamps, that he suggested should be coloured according to price, as well as what the stamps should be made of, were sent to London with a covering letter for Sir Rowland Hill which stipulated that if Chalmers' idea was chosen and used, he should be given due credit.

Patrick Chalmers maintained that although Sir Rowland Hill introduced the new system, he did not come up with any practical plans to make it work. He also maintained that Hill proposed a stamped-folder system or stamped covers. However the House of Commons Select Committee decided that this system was open to fraud and so it was advised that the stamps should be produced using special paper that had interwoven threads running through it, just as Chalmers had suggested. Chalmers' supporters therefore believe that it was this scheme that the government eventually chose to use – not Sir Rowland Hill's.

Patrick Chalmers was convinced, along with many others, that his father's invention saved the Penny Postage Bill from failure and that letters between Sir Rowland Hill and James Chalmers proved this to be the case. Other evidence includes *The Dictionary of National Biography* that credited James Chalmers with the invention of the postage stamp and the 1884 edition of the *Encyclopaedia Britannica* that did the same, although the reference attributing Chalmers as the inventor was later removed.

The dispute as to who created the pre-paid adhesive postage stamp has burned on over the years and it may be that it is now impossible to prove who invented it.

James Chalmers died without being acknowledged for his invention but thanks to his son there is an inscription on his grave in the Dundee burial ground the Howff, that reads, 'Originator of the adhesive postal stamp, which saved the penny postage scheme of 1840 from collapse, rendering it an unqualified success, and which has been adopted throughout the postal systems of the world.'

8. Water, Water Everywhere!

There is another world lurking below Dundee – a network of subterranean and interconnected watercourses.

Number 15 Shore Terrace for example, is home to one of the city's best-kept secrets. Built in 1828, the listed waterfront landmark with its striking terrazzos and Grecian-style columns, is as impressive from the outside as it is on the inside.

Under the building lie the remains of Dundee's eighteenth-century quayside, as well as Packhouse Square, a series of medieval warehouses and storm doors that were constructed in the 1640s. They were built on what was then the sea level as Dundee's shoreline was originally more inland and used to run from the Seagate and the bottom of Castle Street. The docks were then later filled in so that today, Dundee reaches much further into the River Tay and people now walk on what was once water!

Theories suggest that the harbour and packhouses may have been engulfed by a high tidal surge of around 50 feet on November 3 1755, caused when the aftermath of the Lisbon earthquake hit Dundee. When the harbour level was raised as a result, the packhouses were sealed off 14 feet below ground level. Today, this ancient underground world is open to the public on selected dates throughout the year and is well worth a visit; a genuine jewel in the city's heritage crown.

Reminders of Dundee's maritime and mercantile history are everywhere. Just beside Candle Lane in the city centre, is the Sailors' Home and high up on the building are the names of famous sailors. Further along is what was once Seamen's Chapel, featuring the symbol of an anchor and chain above the door, and across the road you'll see Custom House where taxes would have once been paid on imports and exports. Built in 1843, this building is indicative of the trading wealth of Dundee at the time.

Towns and villages often first appear close to sources of fresh water but Dundee's development seems to have been mapped by its connection to it. The city emerged around the ready supply of water from the streams that drained into the Tay basin. Medieval Dundee for example, expanded east and west along the Tay because its spread north was limited by a long stretch of boggy ground called Quaw Bog. In the early fifteenth century the Bog was drained and by the late eighteenth century it provided land and running water for bleaching meadows.

There was also the Tod Burn, the Dens Burn, and its tributary the Wallace Burn, as well as the Scourin' Burn, or cleansing burn as it was known, which probably referred to the process of waulking and scouring yarn.

The Burnhead was located at the top of what is now Commercial Street and was the point where the Dens Burn and the Scourin' Burn met. These combined burns powered the malt and thread mills.

If you know where to look there is still evidence of some of these watercourses, all of which were instrumental to Dundee's growth as a city. For example, the Scourin' Burn can be seen running in a mill lade under the floorboards of a former mill that was built in 1833. This mill is now Dundee's jute museum, Verdant Works. There is a well in the courtyard with a trap door that can be lifted to view the Scourin' Burn.

The Quaw Bog was situated at the confluence of the Scourin' Burn and the Friar Burn. The Bog was drained to allow for the building of The Albert Institute, which is now the McManus Art Gallery and Museum. It opened in 1867 but the design was scaled back when it became clear that the water would make building difficult. Today, unknown to many, an open-walled sump pump operates constantly beneath the Museum to prevent the water rising.

If you listen closely, you can also still hear the Dens Burn running near the far end of the Cowgate – one of the many hidden examples of the fact that Dundee's ancient connection to water still exists today.

Where there were burns, there were also wells. The Ladywell was considered the parent source of Dundee's water supply until 1836. It was located on Bucklemaker Wynd, now Victoria Road, and was dedicated to Dundee's Patron Saint, St Mary. It remained in use until 1872 when the construction of Victoria Road meant it had to be removed.

In 1743, the town council provided an extra supply of watering points including the Dog Well, St Clement's Well, Burnhead Well and the Overgate Well. The only well that can still be seen today is the Overgate Well. It was moved from the Overgate area of the city to Dudhope Castle in 1897.

The wells were public supplies of drinking water, located in places that people needed them. Most of the well spouts were shaped like lions' heads. The Dog Well however, had a dog's head. Wells were also used by the community as meeting places. People gathered there with buckets and stopped to chat to neighbours and to let their horses drink.

However, the wells were eventually removed from use due to concerns about their safety. On analysis, the Ladywell was deemed to be 'a very thoroughly purified sewage from the abattoir next door!'

The Alexandra Fountain however, can still be seen next to the RRS *Discovery* Visitor Centre. This early twentieth-century drinking fountain stands in memory of Queen Alexandra who regularly sailed from Dundee to her native Denmark.

It was presented to the people of Dundee by William Longair the Lord Provost of Dundee at the time, and was moved to its current location in 1992, from its original position nearby.

Incidentally, the Fountain also marks the former site of the Tay Ferry Terminal. The Ferries were known as the 'Fifies', carrying passengers across the River Tay, and traded until 1966 when the Tay Road Bridge opened.

Dundee's liquid assets have been fundamental to its development as a city and are implicitly intertwined in its identity. See what else you can learn about Dundee's watery past!

9. Dundee's Trams

Any visitor to Dundee city centre will notice the old brass tram tracks that weave across the cobblestones. For nearly 100 years, trams made their way around the city's streets.

On 30 August 1877, the first tram operated in Dundee. It was horse-drawn and eight years later, steam engines were introduced. Between 1900 and 1902 the tram system was electrified. The lines extended from the city centre all the way to Broughty Ferry and Monifieth.

Unlike many other cities, Dundee was proud of its trams and they were well-maintained, allowing them to continue in use for a long period of time. Trams were used in Dundee until October 1956 when post-war restrictions led to a steep rise in material costs. The trams were then removed and replaced with more economical buses.

Today, these tram tracks and the Maryfield Tram Depot in the Stobswell area of Dundee, are some of the only remaining evidence in the city that the trams existed. In fact, the Maryfield depot will eventually be home to the Dundee Museum of Transport – just the ticket for those who appreciate a fine set of wheels when they see them! At present the Museum is temporarily located in Market Mews and is raising funds to renovate the former depot.

Led by volunteers from across the city, the Museum aims to restore, preserve and display an ever-changing and diverse collection of transport-related memorabilia and vehicles that represent the heritage of Tayside and beyond. Exhibits include a full-sized licensed replica of Chitty Chitty Bang Bang; a 1930 Angus Council road-roller that is one of just four of its kind that still exist; an 1880s Dundee horse-drawn ambulance; the last-surviving example of an electric double-decker Aberdeen Corporation tram that dates back to 1901

and even Dundee's last-remaining horse-drawn tram from 1887 which, remarkably, was recovered in 2014 from having being used as a summer house in a garden in Perth for between 60 and 100 years.

History such as this is brought to life in Dundee's Museum of Transport. Why not take a stroll down memory lane while you're in Dundee and learn something new about the city's past?

10. The Royal Arch

During the Victorian era, Dundee was a hub of industry and commerce thanks to the arrival of jute manufacturing and its supporting services. With this came considerable wealth and prosperity, and so a civic symbol that represented the Burgh's new-found status was constructed.

In 1844, Queen Victoria and her husband Prince Albert visited the city – the first visit by a British monarch to Dundee since the seventeenth century. Local officials used the opportunity to create a fitting gateway to the city and so a triumphant wooden arch was built at the harbour, indicating the passing from harbour to town. The arch created a magnificent arrival scene for the Royal guests and for the reception ceremonies that followed.

The arch was named the Royal Arch but was also known in Dundee as the Victoria Arch and was intended to be as important to Dundee as the Euston Arch was to London. It stood to highlight Dundee on the world map, drawing attention to the city's role as a seaport and emphasising its international trading ambitions to other countries, particularly India.

The grand arch consisted of a main arch which was surrounded by two smaller side arches and surmounted by two central turrets. It measured 80 feet across, cost between £2,270 and £3,000 to build and was mostly funded by public subscription and donations from harbour trustees. It stood proudly between King William IV Dock and the Earl Grey Dock on the south side of Dock Street, between the junctions of Castle Street and Whitehall Crescent.

In 1849 a competition was held to design a permanent arch to replace the wooden arch and ensure Dundee had a lasting symbol of wealth and prosperity. The entry by John Thomas Rochead, who also designed the Wallace Monument near Stirling, was chosen as the winner.

His quasi-historical, neo-Romanesque design received much criticism from the city's Baltic merchants who felt that it insulted the traders and manufacturers as it didn't accurately express Dundee's international aspirations. However, officials were content with the proposal and so the arch was built. Once the sandstone arch was erected though, it became an iconic symbol and a source of pride for Dundee's citizens.

Sadly, this arch was dynamited in 1964 to make way for the Tay Road Bridge. The rubble was thrown into the King William IV and Earl Grey Docks which in turn were filled in as part of the land reclamation scheme for the Tay Road Bridge.

Today, a cast-bronze model of the Royal Arch can be seen in the city centre, outside the entrance to the Overgate Shopping Centre. A fragment of the original monument can also be seen on display in the Royal Arch bar in Broughty Ferry. The remnant

was recovered in 2010 during works for Dundee's waterfront regeneration project.

These building works exposed the foundations of the once magnificent structure and as a result, the decision was made for the arch to gain pride of place in the new waterfront area by the planting of four trees to mark its former location. The trees will be planted on the placements of the four footings of the former arch and will be accompanied by artwork to depict the stages of the life of the arch.

11. The Tay Whale

Take a trip to the McManus Art Gallery and Museum in Dundee to see a real, full-size skeleton of a whale suspended from the ceiling.

In 1883, a male humpback whale swam into the River Tay, much to the fascination of local residents. At that time, Dundee was the largest whaling port in Britain and the industry was an integral part of Dundee's history, dating back as far as the twelfth century.

Some of the whalers who were home for the winter decided to take the opportunity to hunt on their doorstep instead of in the Arctic where they would have spent most of their time. After several unsuccessful attempts, the whalers managed to harpoon the mammal which then towed two rowing boats and two steamboats as far as Montrose and then to the Firth of Forth. A fierce struggle, combined with strong winds, caused the harpoon lines to snap and the whale broke free.

However, a week later the whale was found dead due to its injuries, six miles off Inverbervie. It was towed to Stonehaven where it was beached. Measuring 40 feet long and weighing 16.5 tons, it attracted much local interest. The fishermen who towed the animal demanded payment for their efforts in bringing the whale back to shore and so the carcass was put up for public auction.

Local entrepreneur and oil merchant John Woods bought the animal for £226 (£11,800 in today's money) and had it moved to Dundee. He exhibited the whale to local residents from his yard and charged them 6d (two and a half pence) and 1/- (five pence), depending on the time of day, to see it. During the fortnight that the whale was on show, 50,000 people paid to see it.

Eventually the whale became too badly decomposed to exhibit. Sir John Struthers, Professor

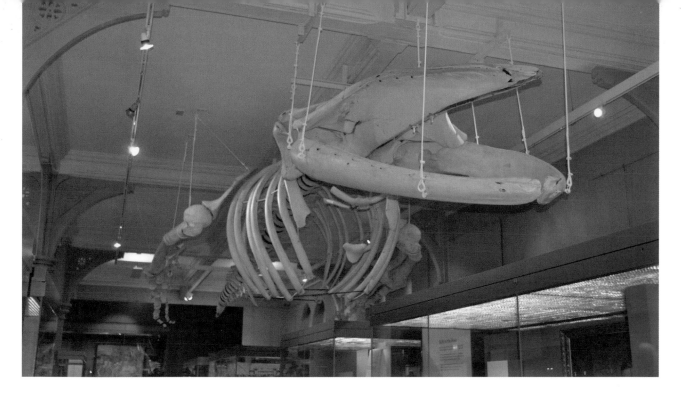

of Anatomy at The University of Aberdeen, was then permitted to dissect the whale in front of a public audience with a military band playing in the background, courtesy of John Woods. In 1889, Sir John Struthers published a complete monograph on the whale.

The skeleton was removed and the carcass was stuffed and reconstructed on a frame so that it could again be taken on a tour, this time around Britain. Seven months after the animal's death, and once Woods made his money, he donated the skeleton to the city of Dundee where it remains to this day.

12. The *Mars* Training Ship

The *Mars* Training ship was a landmark on the River Tay for over fifty years. She was built in 1848 as a warship, saw service during the Crimean War and was brought to the Tay in 1869 where she was refitted as a training ship.

Dundee experienced desperate poverty in the early nineteenth century and many children found themselves orphaned, homeless and forced into a life of theft and criminality. Houses and streets were overcrowded and full of disease and there was no adequate sanitation or safe drinking water.

At the same time the women of Dundee, as cheaper employees, worked in the jute mills while the men and young children were left at home. This led to an increase in drunkenness, lawlessness and family instability. Courts and prisons were stretched to breaking point and there was an increase in orphaned and abandoned children. In 1846 no fewer than 113 children under the age of fourteen were sent to prison.

That was until 1869 when the decision to create a training ship for destitute boys on the River Tay was announced as a way to overcome all of these issues. The *Mars* was decommissioned in 1863 when peace prevailed and she was no longer required. She was then put to use as The *Mars* Training Ship, serving as a floating detention centre and training institution and providing the boys with a life free from poverty, crime and disease as well as the opportunity to learn new skills. She was used until 1929 for the instruction of 350–400 boys at any one time, from Dundee, Glasgow and Edinburgh, in various trades and seamanship.

Training ships provided the Royal Navy with a solution to address its need for a standing body of professional sailors and enabled it to rent out or sell its disbanded wooden ships.

Life on board the *Mars* mirrored that of the Navy.

There was a staff commander, boatswain, master-at-arms, two sailor instructors, a carpenter, a cook and a schoolmaster. The boys were fed, clothed and educated. There was a music room and a gymnasium but strict discipline prevailed. Life was hard and days were long, so much so that more fortunate children in Dundee who were caught misbehaving were often threatened with the yell: 'I'll send ye tae the *Mars*!' The boys were addressed by a number, not a name, which matched their uniform and belongings.

The ship spent the majority of her life moored off Woodhaven in Fife and throughout her time on the River Tay, she was home to over 6,500 boys. She was visible from far and wide, weighing twice the tonnage of the historic HM Frigate *Unicorn*, the oldest British-built warship still afloat, which can be seen today berthed in Dundee's Victoria Dock.

By 1929 however, changing industrial trends meant that there was no longer a need for a training ship and she was sent to the shipbreakers. The boys were put out to farm service in Ireland and to the mining industry in Wales. Sadly, many lost their lives in World War I and they are commemorated today by a memorial at Woodhaven pier in Wormit, Fife – a lovely spot to visit to remember the boys of the *Mars*.

13. Mary Slessor: A Dundee Missionary Abroad

Mary Mitchell Slessor (1848–1915) was a Victorian mill-girl turned missionary who saved the lives of hundreds of native children in Cross River State, Nigeria.

Born in Aberdeen, Mary was the second of seven children and moved to Dundee when she was eleven years old. At that age, because of her father's alcoholism, she was forced to work and found employment in the Baxter's jute mill. Such child workers were known as 'half-timers' as they spent half of their day at the school provided by the mill owners and the other half in employment for the company.

She quickly showed a strong interest in religion and used it as a means of escape from her hard life. She joined the Wishart Church in Dundee and was so inspired that she decided to become a missionary to follow in the footsteps of the legendary missionary and explorer, David Livingstone, and to spread the word of God abroad.

Mary was accepted to go with the Calabar Mission to Nigeria and set sail aboard the SS *Ethiopia*. She was first stationed as a teacher and based with the Efik people. Unlike other missionaries, she chose to live with the tribes and learned their language and their traditions including their beliefs in witchcraft and spiritualism.

Mary made it her aim to end some of the barbaric local practices, such as the killing of twins, and she adopted many Nigerian children who had been left to die. She also fought for the rights of women and set up mission hospitals.

During her missionary work she was faced with constant danger and illness and was sent home a number of times due to bad health. On one of her return visits to Dundee, she brought back a six-month-old twin girl that she had rescued. They stayed in Dundee for over three years before returning to the village of Akpap Okoyong in Nigeria, an area that had claimed the lives of many missionaries. However, Mary stayed with the people of Okoyong for fifteen years teaching them, providing them with medical attention and being a peacemaker. The locals revered her, so much so that they made her a judge of the whole region and she became known as 'the white queen of Okoyong'.

True to her beliefs, Mary lived very simply like the locals in a primitive hut that was infested with roaches, rats, and ants. The other missionaries were unable to relate to the way she lived as she didn't focus on health precautions or cleanliness. Although she did experience ill-health, she outlived most of her missionary co-workers.

As time progressed, Mary's mission became less about religious conversion and more about mercy. Instead of imposing beliefs from Scotland on others, as was custom, she realised that to help the locals and to improve their lives, she had to understand

them as people and be sensitive to their culture and needs. It was this approach that set her apart from her contemporaries.

At the age of fifty-five, Mary moved from the Okoyong area with her seven children to Itu to carry out pioneer work. She died in Nigeria twelve years later in 1915 and was given a state funeral.

Still to this day the people of Calabar hold Mary Slessor in high regard. She is very much part of their history and heritage and is described as the 'Mother of All the Peoples'. One of the main streets in the centre of Calabar is called Mary Slessor Avenue and a traffic roundabout proudly displays a piece of public art erected in her memory.

Today, Mary Slessor is immortalised on the Clydesdale Bank £10 note.

In Dundee, a commemorative bronze plaque in honour of Mary's achievements can be seen outside The Steeple Church. It aims to celebrate the life, and increase the awareness, of one of the city's most extraordinary women.

The Mary Slessor Foundation was set up in 2002 by Dr Lawrie Mitchell and his wife, Eme, the great-great-granddaughter of Ma Eme, who helped Mary Slessor to be accepted by the chiefs during her missionary work. Dr Mitchell and his wife were living and working in Calabar, when they decided that it was important to continue the work of Mary Slessor in order to improve the local economy and to raise self-esteem among the villagers – helping the people of the Calabar district to help themselves.

14. Dundee's Dragon

In the heart of Dundee city's centre you'll find a grand statue of a fearsome dragon. And the story behind it is just as formidable.

The site of Martin's Stone, a Pictish monument that dates back to between 400–850 AD, lies to the north of Dundee near Bridgefoot. Carved with symbols including a dragon, this stone is said to mark the spot where a dragon was slain.

Legend has it that a local farmer lived with his nine beautiful daughters in the village of Pitempton. One day, after hours of working on the land, he sent his youngest daughter to a local well for water. When she did not return, he sent another daughter to look for her. The second daughter did not return and so he sent another. This continued until all nine of his daughters were missing.

Sensing something untoward, he went to find his daughters and was met by a gruesome dragon beside their bodies. The father ran for his life and managed to tell his neighbours what he had seen. They were outraged and banded together to kill the beast. A young man called Martin, who had loved the farmer's eldest daughter, eventually killed the dragon. The spot where the beast fell is marked with what is now known as Martin's Stone.

As a result of the tragedy, the well at Pitempton was named the Nine Maidens' Well. St Martin's Stone was erected by the citizens to commemorate the event and a church nearby was dedicated to St Martin on 18 May 1249. The area where the dragon was slain was named 'Strike-Martin' which subsequently became Strathmartin, a name that today you will see used for street names and regions throughout Dundee and beyond.

Of course, there are a number of different versions of this story and various interpretations have evolved

over the years. Perhaps an explanation lies in the Pictish symbols that are carved on St Martin's Stone alongside the depiction of the dragon. What do these mean? What are they trying to tell us? So far, nobody has been able to work out what they represent.

However, to honour the legend and the mystery that surrounds it, Dundee's Dragon was created in 1994 by artist Tony Marrow from a maquette by Alistair Smart. The bronze sculpture is just one example of over 100 pieces of public art that can be found across the city. See how many you can spot during your visit to Dundee.

15. William Wallace in the City of Discovery

According to Dundee's ancient historical documents, one of the most famous names in the war for Scottish independence in the thirteenth and fourteenth centuries has a strong connection with Dundee.

It is said that William Wallace (1270–1305), the man who struck the first blow against the English Monarchy in the thirteenth century, is believed to have completed his education in Dundee in 1291.

Wallace attended a church school which was led by William Mydford, the Vicar of Dundee. He was educated by an order of Knights who had learned their trade in the Far East. However, while carrying out his studies, an event took place that was to shape his future and the story has become one of the legends of Dundee.

A fight broke out between Wallace and one of his fellow pupils named Selby, who also happened to be the son of the English Governor or Constable of the Castle and Town of Dundee. In 1291, the English King, Edward I, gained control of Scotland and installed English Sheriffs in all Scottish castles.

Selby offended Wallace, professing that his low rank in life did not entitle him to carry a dagger and chastised him for wearing green – a sign of being gentry. Wallace was so outraged by the remarks that he drew his dagger and stabbed his classmate to death.

Wallace was then forced to flee Dundee. He left through the West Port and made his way to Perth, where he planned to take refuge with his uncle in the Carse of Gowrie. The English soldiers pursued him but when Wallace made it to Longforgan, he is said to have sat down to rest on a husking stone at the door of a crofter whose wife took pity on him.

It is thought that the crofter woman disguised Wallace in one of her russet gowns and headdresses so that when the English soldiers arrived, they did not recognise him and continued on with their search.

Another version of the story tells how Wallace sat on the grindstone and when the crofters came home, they gave him a glass of milk and he continued on his way.

By then, Wallace was a marked man and he gathered patriots who had refused to take the oath of allegiance to Edward and began to form what would become the Scottish army. His attack on the garrison at Ayr, his crossing of the boundary into Lanarkshire and his slaying of Heselrig, the English Sheriff, signified the beginning of the War of Independence.

However, as with any local legend, the story of Wallace's time in Dundee should be read with a degree of caution. Accounts of Wallace having murdered Selby didn't appear until the 1700s – around 400 years after the event was said to have taken place.

Moreover, the accounts are based on poetry written 100 or more years after Wallace died. If he did murder Selby, though, it would have been Wallace's first kill.

What is known for certain is that Wallace returned to Dundee several years later to reclaim the city. He began the infamous siege of the Castle of Dundee but left mid-way through to fight the Battle of Stirling Bridge, which was immortalised in the film Braveheart.

Remarkably, the grinding stone upon which Wallace is said to have sat was preserved by the farmer's descendants for nearly 600 years and is now housed in the McManus Art Gallery and Museum.

Whatever you believe, it could be argued that if Wallace had not been sent to study in Dundee, he might not have been set on the path that eventually led him to his victory at Stirling.

16. The Castle of Dundee

Not much is known about the Castle of Dundee but it is thought to have occupied a site on the hill at the top of Castle Street, in the centre of town next to where St Paul's Cathedral now stands. Originally the hill rose straight from the tide-line but land reclamation in the late eighteenth century pushed the sea back from the rock.

It is believed that the Castle of Dundee existed by 1290 at the latest. It was one of the principal fortresses in Scotland and played a prominent role in Scotland's War of Independence against Edward I of England and his son, Edward II. For example, William Wallace is said to have struck the first blow for Scottish independence in the Castle of Dundee, c.1288 and he laid siege to the Castle in 1297, before the Battle of Stirling Bridge.

In 1296 and 1303, the Castle was captured by the English. King Edward I of England visited the Castle both times and made repairs then King Robert the Bruce re-captured the castle in 1313 before, some say, destroying it.

Others believe that the Castle was destroyed under the instruction of William Wallace or that it was dismantled by Edward Bruce when he attempted to concentrate the whole of the Scottish forces at Bannockburn.

Whatever the cause of the Castle's demise, it is known that by 1318 the Castle of Dundee had disappeared from history, leaving a trail of mystery in its wake.

SITE OF CASTLE OF DUNDEE
DESTROYED *CIR* 1314 — NEAR THIS SPOT
WILLIAM WALLACE STRUCK THE FIRST BLOW
FOR SCOTTISH INDEPENDENCE *CIR* 1288
HERE WAS THE BIRTHPLACE OF
ADMIRAL DUNCAN 1731
VICTOR OF CAMPERDOWN 1797
IN HOUSE ADJOINING
THE CHEVALIER DE ST. GEORGE
SPENT THE NIGHT OF 6TH JANUARY 1716
AFTER PUBLIC ENTRY INTO DUNDEE

17. The Town House

Dundee's Town House was a large arcade building which replaced the sixteenth-century Tolbooth. It was situated in the Seagate and a cobbled cross at the foot of Peter Street marks the spot where it once stood. It boasted a clock-tower which chimed the quarter hour during a period when very few people owned a watch.

The Town House was designed by the leading Scottish architect of the time, William Adam and was built between 1732 and 1734. Featuring seven bays, it was regarded as one of the most distinguished buildings in Scotland. The ground floor was occupied by an arcade of shops and a bank, and the upper floors housed a court jail and the original Burgh Chambers.

It became known as The Pillars because of the arcades, and it was steeped in history. The Town House was the site of public executions and it saw an attempt by the Jacobites to return power under Bonnie Prince Charlie in 1745. At the end of the eighteenth century it hosted public protests inspired by the French Revolution and in 1803, when Napoleon threatened invasion, the Provost of Dundee assembled volunteers at the Town House. In 1832, rioters tried to set fire to the building in protest at the Tories.

Against much public opposition, the Town House was demolished in 1932 as part of modernisation developments. Many local shopkeepers erected models of the Town House in its memory and today, a model of the building can be seen outside the Pillars Bar in Crichton Street. There is also a commemorative clock high up on one of the buildings of Gardyne's Land, the oldest surviving set of residential buildings in Dundee. The clock reads 'Memory is Time'.

18. Gates and Ports

A town wall was built around Dundee in the late fifteenth century and each road into town had a port. These served as control points where traders entering the town had to pass and pay a fee.

At one time, Dundee had seven ports leading to the city. As the town grew, the gates were moved to new positions and many of the ports gave their names to the areas in which they were situated. These names are still in use today.

The Seagate (originally Seagait) for example, was one of the first areas of settlement in Dundee, dating from at least the eleventh century, and it is one of the city's oldest surviving streets. Gates were originally spelled 'Gaits' which meant 'thoroughfare' in Scots. The Seagate was so-called because the street linked the city directly with the river. The original shore of the River Tay was located at the east end of the Seagate and the sixteenth century Seagate Port was located near Sugarhouse Wynd.

The Murraygate (originally Murraygait) is also one

of Dundee's oldest streets, dating from the early fourteenth century. The Murraygate Port, which no longer exists, was removed in the mid-seventeenth century. The Murraygate is thought to have been named after Thomas Randolph, Earl of Moray, a companion and fellow soldier of William Wallace and Robert the Bruce.

The Cowgate (originally Cowgait) is so-called because the Town Herd drove cattle along this street in medieval times. Today, the city's only surviving town port is located there. Known as the Cowgait Port or Wishart's Arch, it has its own unique history. When the plague-stricken were removed from Dundee, the Protestant Reformer, George Wishart (1513–1546), who had been banned from Dundee by church authorities, famously climbed on top of the Arch to preach to both the healthy inside the city and to the plague victims who were forced to live outside the city walls. The dates surrounding this claim however, mean that this piece of history may in fact be hearsay.

The Wellgate (originally Wellgait) area of Dundee is built on the site of the old Wellgate which used to be the street leading to the Ladywell that was dedicated to Dundee's Patron Saint, St Mary. The Wellgate Port dated from the seventeenth century and was likely to have been built to secure the area and to create a boundary between the Dundee aristocracy and those living in Rotten Row, otherwise known as the Hilltown. Originally, a number of thatched working-class houses were built on both sides of the main road that ran through the Hilltown, giving rise to the name Rotten Row. These houses were mainly occupied by Bonnetmakers – Dundee was the first town in Scotland to have an incorporated trade of Bonnetmakers.

The Overgate (originally Overgait) was once a busy medieval route in and out of Dundee and is now occupied by a modern shopping centre. It was originally known as Argyll's Gait because it provided a route from the former Marketgate into the country, via a mansion house called Argyll's Lodging. The name

Overgate means 'the upper way'.

Similarly, the Nethergate (originally Nethergait) means 'the lower way' as it led along the river to the villages of Westfield and Springfield. It was formerly known as the Flukergate in reference to a type of flat fish that was found in the River Tay. The Flukergate Port became the Nethergate Port in the sixteenth century, located near the junction of South Tay Street.

The Marketgait existed from the thirteenth century and eventually became known as the High Street. As the name suggests, it was the town's market place and by the fifteenth century, the Tron, Tolbooth and Mercat Cross were all situated here.

In 1746, following the Battle of Culloden, the town council demolished the town walls, except of course for the Wishart Arch which was kept as a memorial of days gone by.

19. The Mercat Cross and The Tron

The Scots term 'mercat cross' means, quite simply, a market cross. Found in many Scottish towns and cities, market crosses were the centre of mercantile life. They also often became focal points for local gatherings.

Dundee's Mercat Cross dates back to 1586 and was originally located in the High Street. Earlier sites included the Seagate and later opposite the top of Crichton Street. The Cross is octagonal in structure and carved from stone. It features a resin-bronze unicorn, sculpted in the 1960s, that bears a shield with Royal Arms. The unicorn is raised on the original carved shaft that was designed by the Master Mason, John Mylne.

In 1777, the Cross had to be removed from the west end of the High Street because it was obstructing horse-drawn traffic. It was moved at least once more before being returned to its current location outside The Steeple Church as part of the redevelopment of the Overgate area of the city.

Meanwhile, although no longer in existence, the Tron or public weighing beam was erected in 1363–1364 in the Marketgait area of the city. As in most towns, traders seeking to sell goods in Dundee were required to have them weighed. In 1560 a weigh house, where the town's weights and measures were kept, was built on the west side of St Clement's Church.

Both the Mercat Cross and the Tron were early symbols of Dundee's success as a hub of trade and commerce.

20. Gardyne's Land

Quietly unassuming and often overlooked, Gardyne's Land is the oldest surviving set of residential buildings in Dundee, dating back to the mid-sixteenth century.

Located at number 71 High Street, the structure is a complex of three different but linked buildings around an inner courtyard. At the centre of the site sits a merchant's house from which the area took its name. Originally, this house was built for a wealthy trader and the attention to detail and sophisticated architecture is said to be indicative of Dundee's status and prosperity at the time. The house is tucked away behind more modern buildings on the High Street and is accessible via Gray's Close.

The building is dated circa 1560 and true to Dundee's maritime heritage, much of the timber that was used in its construction was from the Baltic. It was first owned by John Gardyne, a name which is thought to derive from the old Scots word for garden. This central building is surrounded by two town houses, which date from around 1640 and 1790, as well as a Victorian retail outlet from 1865 and a billiard hall from c.1820.

The buildings have changed significantly over time and little of their original interiors still exist. However, a panelled room dating from 1720 and the workshops of a watchmaker and a bagpipe maker survive. These have been thoughtfully restored, along with the rest of the buildings, by the Tayside Building Preservation Trust and a small exhibition is open to the public.

Look out for the commemorative clock of the old Town House that sits high up on the exterior façade of Gardyne's Land.

21. The Submarine Memorial

Most people know about Dundee's World War II Memorial which sits proudly atop the Law – the plug of an extinct volcano. However, not quite so many people have visited the city's International Submarine Memorial at Victoria Dock in Dundee harbour.

Unveiled in 2009, it commemorates the six British, Dutch, Norwegian and Russian submarines that were lost while on patrol from Dundee during the Second World War. It is dedicated to the 296 sailors and commandos who were killed on operations from the base at Dundee which was the home port of the Royal Navy's 9th Submarine Flotilla, from 1940 to 1945. In fact, Dundee was also the base of the 2nd Submarine Flotilla in 1939.

A unique international force, the Flotilla was made up of British units as well as Free-French, Dutch, Norwegian and Polish crews after their countries had been overrun by the Nazis. Russian submarine crews were also based in Dundee in the summer of 1944.

Dundee-based submarines took part in some of the most dangerous naval operations of the War. They patrolled far beyond the Arctic Circle to protect convoys carrying much-needed war supplies to the Soviet Union and they patrolled perilously close to enemy naval bases in Nazi occupied Norway, watching for signs that enemy warships were sailing to attack Allied shipping. They intercepted U-boats making for the Atlantic convoy routes and they landed secret agents, Special Operations Executive saboteurs, Combined Operations commandos, weapons and supplies for resistance groups in occupied Norway.

Created by artists Paul Grime and Jeremy Cunningham, the submarine memorial was funded by Dundee City Council and The Unicorn Property Group. It honours the gallantry and commemorates the sacrifice of the men who undertook remarkable

acts of navigation, seamanship and warfare during World War II.

    Three remembrance ceremonies are held every year at the memorial: the Russian Victory Day Ceremony on 9 May, the International Remembrance Service in September and a short wreath laying ceremony on Remembrance Sunday.

22. Dundee's Other Ship

Almost every visitor to Dundee has heard about Captain Scott's famous polar exploration ship, the RRS *Discovery*, but fewer people know about Dundee's HM Frigate *Unicorn*.

Now preserved as an historic ship and visitor attraction, *Unicorn* is the oldest British-built warship still afloat. She was built as a 46-gun sailing frigate for the Royal Navy in Chatham and was launched in 1824. She took nearly two years and almost 1,000 oak trees to build.

The ship was used as a powder store on the Thames and was brought to Dundee in 1873 as a drill ship for training and for use as the Royal Naval Volunteer Reserve administrative headquarters. She was nearly scrapped when the decision was made for the dock, in which she was originally berthed, to be filled in. However, she was reprieved and moved to Dundee's Victoria Dock in 1962.

Today, she is one of the six oldest surviving ships in the world and is Scotland's only preserved warship. Incredibly, she is also the most completely original ship in the entire world to have survived from the Golden Age of Sail.

The *Unicorn* figurehead that can be seen on the ship wears the naval coronet with alternating sails and stern castles. It supports a gilded cartouche that bears the Royal Arms.

On board, the ship is a treasure-trove of memorabilia and is filled with dark, low compartments. It contains many of its original warfare features from its launch including cannon, hammocks, the mess area, the officers' wardroom and the Captain's cabin – complete with removable doors for ease of movement during the height of action.

The ship is unusual in that she has spent almost her entire working life in one port and has been in Dundee

for 141 years. She predates some of the most historic buildings in the city centre and is a fundamental part of Dundee's heritage.

HM Frigate *Unicorn* is maintained and run by the *Unicorn* Preservation Society and is open to the public as a museum at her berth in Victoria Dock.

23. World Record Seaplane Flight

On 6 October 1938, the world distance record for a seaplane was set – a record that is still held to this day.

The Maia flying boat, piloted by A S Wilcockson, took off from the River Tay, carrying the Mercury – a small, long-range seaplane. The Mercury was positioned on top of the larger flying boat for assisted take off. At six miles outside Dundee, the planes separated and the Mercury continued towards its destination. It touched down on the River Orange in Alexander Bay, South-West Africa and in so doing, set a seaplane distance record of 6,045 miles.

The Mercury and Maia together formed a piggyback aircraft called the Short-Mayo Composite which used the power of both aircraft to climb to operational altitude before the Mercury was released. Having both aircraft take off together reduced fuel consumption, leaving the maximum amount of fuel for the smaller aircraft, the Mercury, to continue its long journey.

About halfway through the flight, D C Bennett, the Captain of the Mercury, feared that he was running low on fuel but managed to complete the journey, descending through a cloud of flamingos as he came in to land. Captain Bennett was the famed founder and Commander of the Royal Air Force Pathfinder Force during the Second World War.

A memorial to the epic flight, courtesy of Captain Bennett's wife, can be seen on Dundee's Riverside next to the RSS *Discovery* Visitor Centre.

COMMEMORATION OF THE 1908 FLIGHT OF CAPTAIN BENNETT FROM THE TAY ESTUARY TO SOUTH WEST AFRICA

24. Dundee's Time Capsule

Dundee is home to a unique First World War time capsule that was put together and sealed by postal workers in the city in 1921. Known as the Dundee Postal War Memorial Shrine, the lead-lined oak casket bears a plaque instructing that it should only be opened by the postmaster in the presence of the Lord Provost on 4 August 2014 – the 100th anniversary of the start of the conflict.

A grand ceremony was held to open the historic shrine and reveal its contents. As Dundee no longer has a postmaster, the Royal Mail delivery director in charge of postal collection and delivery services, led the proceedings, assisted by the Lord Provost and a representative of Dundee High School who are now the owners of the 1921 Post Office building. Amateur historian Janice Kennedy, whose family history research was responsible for discovering the historic capsule, also provided a watchful eye.

Inside the treasure chest was a whole host of memorabilia including sealed letters to the current Lord Provost and Postmaster from their counterparts of the time, newspaper clippings, a copy of the 1921 *Post Office* magazine, photographs of soldiers, scenes of Dundee, postmen and visits by Princess Mary in 1920 and Winston Churchill in 1921, an edition of the *Dundee Courier* and the *Scottish Swimming Association Handbook* from 1921, as well as an essay on the League of Nations, addressed to the youngest member of the education authority in 2014.

A total of 240 Dundee postal employees served in World War I. Sadly, thirty-six died.

The time capsule offers a chance for visitors to step back in time and gain a fascinating insight into the role that Dundee postal workers played throughout the First World War. It gives Dundee a unique artefact by which to honour and remember all those who gave so

much for the future welfare of their city and its people. The time capsule and its contents are available to view on request at The Barrack Street Museum Collections Unit.

NORTH DUNDEE

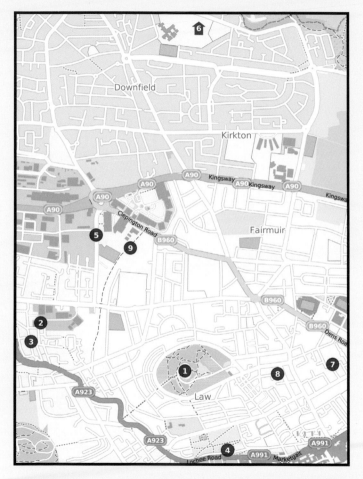

1. The Law Tunnel
2. The Leaning Tower of Dundee
3. She Toon
4. The Time Gun
5. Scotland's Boxing Champion
6. The Sidlaws
7. St Salvador's Episcopal Church
8. Dundee's Unsung World War II Heroes
9. The Miley

1. The Law Tunnel

The Dundee Law is the city's most distinctive landmark. The word 'law' is a lowland Scots term meaning hill. At 572 feet high, the Dundee Law is in fact the plug of an extinct volcano.

Most have no idea, however, that there is a railway tunnel running straight through it!

The tunnel was part of the Dundee to Newtyle railway line that opened in 1831 and was one of the first passenger trains in Scotland and the first commercial railway in northern Scotland.

The line ran through the 984 feet by 98 feet tunnel that was dug into the Dundee Law at an altitude of over 300 feet, creating a unique railway for its time.

The railway boasted several unusual features, one of which was the 'up-and-over' method of crossing the Sidlaw hills – a range of hills of volcanic origin that lie a few miles north of Dundee.

The method worked by placing three stationary steam engines at the top of three inclines known as the Law, Balbeuchly and Hatton inclines. The train carriages and wagons were pulled up or lowered down by rope on a sloping path called an incline plane.

At the top of the Law, the rope was detached and the train was coupled to a horse which then pulled it through the Law Tunnel.

Initially, the coaches and wagons were pulled by horses over the intervening level stretches of line. On the level section of the railway where the horses pulled the coaches, speed was often accelerated by hoisting a wagon sheet on a pole attached to the carriage. Because of this, it was often said that a railway train with a sail once ran from Dundee. When there was no wind, the horses had to do all the work themselves. Later, the horses were replaced by steam locomotives.

In the 1870s, the Law Tunnel was at the centre of a major heist when a large quantity of the Lord Provost's

silver went missing and was eventually found stashed away in the tunnel!

The railway was closed in the 1860s and the tunnel was then used for everything from a mushroom farm to a bomb shelter and even a rubbish tip. The tunnel was officially closed in the 1980s when the two main entrances were built over. The southern entrance was located below St David's High Kirk in what was once a village drying field and later a tennis court. This area is now Kinghorne Road and has been completely built upon with houses. There is, however, a manhole cover in the area that provides the only known surviving access to the tunnel.

Today, a Dundee artist is striving to have this unique location reopened as a world-class visitor attraction, focusing on the history of the site and its importance to Dundee.

2. The Leaning Tower of Dundee

The Cox Brothers, James, William, Thomas and George, were among some of the wealthiest and best-known jute manufacturers in Dundee. In the nineteenth century, demand for jute and linen brought great prosperity to the city because of the shortage of cotton during the American Civil War. To keep up with demand, many jute barons including the Cox Brothers, invested in modern buildings and machinery.

Cox's Stack is a grand example of one such investment. The 282-feet high chimney-stack, which now leans slightly to one side, is a lasting legacy of the impact that the Cox family had on the city and an enduring memory of Dundee's connection with the jute industry. The lean is caused by the existence of an underground chamber in the foundations of the stack. As a precaution, this chamber was filled in with concrete in the 1990s to prevent the chimney from collapsing completely.

James Cox inherited a weaving business with 280 looms from his father. He formed a partnership with his brothers and went on to turn Cox Brothers into the largest jute production site in the world at that time. The business was known as Camperdown Works and its success tripled the population of Lochee, the area of Dundee in which it was located.

At around 30 acres, Camperdown Works was unique in Dundee in that it was the only works that was set out around its own railway siding. The branch of the Newtyle railway that opened in 1861 carried finished jute products to the harbour. The Works was also grand in scale, employing 5,000 people – more than any other mill in the city or in Britain.

There were fifty-seven boilers at the Works and the smoke from the manufacturing process was carried in underground channels to feed the single chimney-stack. Designed and built between 1861 and 1868 by the youngest of the Cox brothers, engineer George Cox and architect James McLaren, the landmark stack was nicknamed Cox's Stack after the mill's owners.

The stack features horizontal bands and patterns of red and yellow bricks. More than a million bricks were used to build the chimney at a cost of around £6,000. It symbolised the fact that Camperdown Works had been planned from scratch by the Cox brothers with guidance from the textile mill engineer, Peter Carmichael. It was deliberately tall and was built so that it could be seen above the Law – the plug of an extinct volcano – and by those approaching the city from Broughty Ferry.

The real purpose of the chimney however, was humanitarian. Being so tall, it helped to keep the air at ground level cleaner for the mill workers. In fact, Cox's mills were pioneering for their time. They were modern and used high-tech machinery and they employed medical staff as well as teachers for their

child workers, known as half-timers. Although the wages were lower than in other mills in the city, the Cox brothers looked after their staff by providing public parks and buildings for recreation and enjoyment. Lochee Park for example, was donated to the city by the Cox Brothers in 1890.

Camperdown Works closed in 1981 but because it has been recognised as the finest remaining example of a Victorian mill building in Britain, and is home to the tallest surviving example of an industrial chimney in Scotland, Dundee's local authority saved it from demolition. It has now been converted into modern flats and Cox's Stack still stands as an enduring monument to the contribution that the Cox brothers made to the city.

3. She Toon

Anyone who reads anything about Dundee will know that its history is inextricably linked with the jute industry. In fact, so successful was the industry in the city that at one point, Dundee was home to the richest square mile in Europe.

However, unlike so many other cities, Dundee employed a large number of women in its factories. Women were cheaper to employ, commanding at least half the rates in Victorian times as men. Boys were hired after school and then fired when they turned eighteen and were due a full male wage. It is true that the jute industry generated huge prosperity for Dundee, but it also brought with it intense poverty, with jute workers' wages being the lowest in the United Kingdom for textile workers.

At a time when society dictated that women belonged in the home and that when they were married they were expected to give up work, Dundee bucked the trend. A large percentage of the city's workforce was both female and married.

This role reversal meant that it became difficult for men to source work and young boys found themselves unemployed after completing their apprenticeships. Because of this, men found themselves idle, with no sense of purpose.

Profound levels of male drunkenness ensued as did the emergence of the 'Dundee woman'. Known to be strong-willed and loud due to the noise of the machinery in the mills, they also used snuff to clear their noses of the jute dust.

The women could also be easily identified because of their torn lips – biting the ends of the jute caused their lips to split and their hands the same. The women developed their own sign language to communicate over the noise in the mills and a hierarchy evolved among them. Weavers were seen

as superior, spinners were next and the sack-sewers followed. Last of course, were the child workers or half-timers, often called the 'puir wee shifters'.

As a result of this female employment, Dundee had a high proportion of women who were able to earn their own keep and didn't have to marry to survive. Many women in Dundee therefore did not marry until much later than their contemporaries in other Scottish towns.

Dundee's jute-mill women were so important that in the early twentieth century, the city was often referred to as the 'Woman's Town' and later as the 'She Toon'. By way of tribute to this, a statue of a jute-mill woman can be seen on the High Street in the Lochee area of the city.

The bronze statue pays homage to the area's jute-mill past and aims to give the people of Lochee and of Dundee, something to inspire them to be proud of their heritage and of their community. It was the brainchild of local woman and former weaver Stella Carrington, on whom the sculpture is modelled. Hanging onto the statue's coat-tails is a child worker, reflecting the high number of children who were employed in Dundee's mills.

Indeed, such has been the influence of Dundee's women throughout history that a trail was created, allowing visitors to walk in the footsteps of some of these great women.

Dundee Women's Trail is the perfect route for anyone who wants to know more about how the city's women have shaped the arts, education, industry, business, health and social care of Dundee – and the world. It provides a fascinating history of twenty-five Dundee women, including artists, trade unionists, social reformers, suffragettes, and a marine engineer, all of whom lived extraordinary lives. They are commemorated with bronze plaques around the city which are located on buildings that are closely associated with each of the women. Why not take the opportunity to learn about Professor of Midwifery and Gynaecology, Margaret Fairlie (1891–1963), who pioneered the use of radium for cancer, or Jean Thomson (1881–1940), Scotland's first policewoman, to name but two?

4. The Time Gun

Dundee's time gun was inaugurated to the sound of rapturous applause in 1872. It marked the spirit and progress of the city and, for the first time, enabled its residents to be guided by one uniform time.

Up until then, the lack of an exact time was the root cause of much anxiety and trouble throughout the city. Provost Yeaman recognised this and set about making it possible for Dundee to have its own time gun, stating that, 'There is nothing more valuable in a manufacturing and commercial city than exactness to time.'

Setting itself apart from rival cities, Dundee was only the second city in Scotland to obtain a time gun: Edinburgh was the first. The gun itself was built into an embankment at Dudhope Castle and was fired daily at 1pm. The original gun was cast in 1813 and saw service on board ships at the close of the Napoleonic war.

The gun was a 12-pounder and used 2lbs of gunpowder. Next to the gun was a wooden hut that housed the apparatus which was used to fire the gun, including the exploder, galvanometer and clock. The time of the clock was regulated approximately as a guide to the gunner. This was his signal to begin turning the handle of the detonating mechanism 15 seconds before the firing current that set the gun off was expected to arrive.

Although the flash of the gun gave the exact time, the sound of the explosion travelled at a rate of 1 mile every 5 seconds. This meant that it was actually later than 1pm by the time the gun's sound reached the outermost parts of Dundee.

The time to which the gun was regulated was obtained by monitoring the sun over the meridian at the observatory in Carlton Hill in Edinburgh. The process of firing the gun and keeping it connected to the exact time was rather complex.

The clock in the Edinburgh observatory was regulated to the one-hundredth part of a second each day at one

o'clock. Every movement of the pendulum transmitted a current of electricity along a wire through a series of clocks in Edinburgh, one of which was used to fire the time gun at Edinburgh Castle.

The series of clocks was located in front of the Register Office and in the General Post Office. One of the clocks in the Post Office was responsible for transmitting the current of electricity that fired the time gun in Dundee.

By adjustment of the machinery, about one and a half minutes before 1pm, the clock cut the connection of the wire with the telegraphic instrument. Exactly at the hour, a beat of the clock came into contact with the local battery from which the electric current was transmitted to Dundee.

Following complaints, however, the gun was silenced in February 1916. It was said to have been disturbing the soldiers in the nearby Dundee Royal Infirmary who were recovering from shell-shock as a result of their service in World War I.

From 1924 onwards, the gun was fired only on Armistice Day and New Year's Day until 1936, and was removed some time later.

The disused gun can still be seen today in the grounds of Dudhope Castle.

5. Scotland's Boxing Champion

With eighteen children in the family, the McTaggarts from the Dens Road area of Dundee were always a force to be reckoned with. However, it was Richard McTaggart, born in 1935, who made sure the family's name went down in history.

His boxing career began in the old Belmont Boxing Club on Blackness Road where his father sent him and his brother to stop them from constantly 'scrapping'. But it was national service that really gave McTaggart the opportunity to shine. There, he found a mentor who helped uncover his potential and convinced him to take up the sport again after he had given up because he felt he wasn't getting anywhere.

In 1956, McTaggart travelled to Melbourne to represent his country in the first Olympics in the Southern hemisphere. With his trademark crew cut and white boots, he beat Harry Kurschat of West Germany and lifted Scotland's only boxing gold to date. He was also awarded the Val Barker trophy, presented to the most stylish boxer of the Games.

However, McTaggart was never officially recognised at the time of his success. When he left the RAF, he became a pest-control consultant, earning him the nickname 'The Rat Catcher', and then he went on to work for Rolls-Royce. Dundonians, adored him though and thousands lined the streets to welcome him home from Melbourne. Local boxers tied ropes to his old Morris car and pulled it, with McTaggart inside, from the train station up to his parents' house in Dens Road, while huge crowds cheered them on.

McTaggart took part in two more Olympic Games, becoming the first British boxer to compete in three Olympiads. He reached the quarter-final stage of the Tokyo Games in 1964, won 610 of 634 amateur bouts throughout his career and amassed 32 cups, 57 plaques and 49 medals – an incredible record.

McTaggart was crowned Commonwealth Champion in 1958, European Champion in 1961 and collected silver at the 1962 Commonwealth Games. He also won three ABA lightweight titles and two light-welterweight belts. He served for many years as the Honorary Director of Coaching to successive Scottish Commonwealth Games boxers, and was awarded an MBE in 2002.

Today, McTaggart is considered by many as Britain's finest amateur boxer. An impressive nine-foot statue of the boxer himself can be viewed on request at the St Francis ABC Boxing Gym, subject to availability.

6. The Sidlaws

A few miles north of Dundee there is a range of hills of volcanic origin, known as the Sidlaws. They stretch for thirty miles from Perth to north-east Forfar and offer visitors the perfect chance to blow away the cobwebs and indulge in a spot of hill walking.

Law is a lowland Scots word meaning a hill which rises sharply from the surrounding land. The Sid part of the Sidlaws is thought to derive from the Scottish Gaelic 'sidhe' which means 'fairy' or 'sacred' and is believed to refer to the prehistoric cairns that are still visible on some of the hills. According to folklore these cairns, or man-made stacks of stones, are home to supernatural beings.

The main peaks of the Sidlaws are Ark Hill and King's

Seat, while the highest of the Sidlaws is Craigowl Hill. Points of interest include Dunsinane Hill, mentioned in Shakespeare's play *Macbeth*, and Auchterhouse Hill, which was the site of an ancient hill fort. At the base of the Sidlaws there is also a memorial to Syd Scroggie (1919–2006), a local author, poet and blind climbing enthusiast who lost a leg and his sight during service in World War II.

Walkers will also occasionally be lucky enough to see beautifully coloured agates. These semi-precious quartz gemstones formed over millions of years in cavities (originally gas bubbles) in the volcanic lava in the hills. Over time, they have been weathered out of the rock in the surrounding fields.

With a range of walks of varying distances to choose from, the Sidlaws offer panoramic views over Dundee and nearby areas and are well worth the effort!

7. St Salvador's Episcopal Church

Dundee's grand St Salvador's Church is a sight not to be missed. As Scotland's finest and most important Victorian Gothic Revival church, it features a glorious painted interior with colourful panelled reredos, stencilled walls and a fine wrought-iron, gilded choir screen.

St Salvador is Latin for 'Holy Saviour', a popular ancient Scottish name for churches. The church was founded in 1856 by Bishop Alexander Penrose Forbes and the Reverend James Nicolson, later Dean of Brechin. It was built for the poor, neglected mill workers of the Hilltown area of Dundee and therefore has a long historical connection to the city.

The Church was considered a unique masterpiece of the leading church architect George Frederick Bodley. It was specifically designed to give the mill workers a break from their hard lives and because of this, the interior is a celebration of gold and colour, boasting splendour and richness. As such, St Salvador's is unique in Scotland.

The Church is open to all and the entrance is located on Carnegie Street. Today, St Salvador's operates as a small, friendly congregation and still works to fulfil its original mission of providing aid to the city's poor by running one of Dundee's busiest food banks.

8. Dundee's Unsung World War II Heroes

The Currans, a working class couple from Dundee, were paid the grand total of one pound for their help in exposing a Nazi agent living in the city during World War II.

In order to protect them and their family from the Germans hunting them down, the Currans were told never to speak about what they had been involved in. As such, their heroism was never publically recognised. However, on the seventieth anniversary of the outbreak of World War II, their daughter chose to break her silence to let the world hear her parents' extraordinary story.

Mr and Mrs Curran exposed the work of Jessie Jordan, a woman who once ran a hairdresser's shop on Dundee's Kinloch Street. The business though, was a ruse. Jordan's real job was that of a Nazi spy working for the German Government as part of an international network preparing for war.

Mother-of-four Mary Curran, was Jordan's cleaner and she took an instant dislike to her boss. Little did she imagine that, while cleaning, she would go on to find maps behind the cash register, as well as one sticking out of the linoleum, that showed the River Tay with a Zeppelin overhead.

The Curran's reported their findings to the police who eventually agreed to contact MI5. The agency was aware of Jessie Jordan but they did not know about her shop in Kinloch Street until they heard Mary Curran's evidence. The shop's address was then added to the mail-watch on Jessie Jordan and it began to uncover some incriminating evidence from the United States.

Some of the letters that were intercepted included one from a Nazi agent who was codenamed 'Crown' and was working in New York. The letters contained plans to assassinate a United States Colonel, steal the strategy for the American fleet in the Atlantic, and blame it all on Russia.

Incredibly, as a result of the intelligence from the Currans, British and American agents joined together to intercept and demolish the spy ring in which Jessie Jordan was involved.

Although the Currans never did see the day when their efforts in World War II were publicly recognised, their daughter wanted to tell her parents' story to ensure that the names of Dundee's real-life spy catchers went down in history as local heroes.

9. The Miley

The Miley Road Urban Wildlife Reserve runs along the east side of Lochee on a section of the old Newtyle to Dundee railway line.

Entirely man-made, it was developed by the Scottish Wildlife Trust in 1992 and provides a secluded haven for wildlife in the city. It has become an area of local importance as a green corridor site and is often used as part of educational programmes.

The reserve supports grassland, tall herb communities, wild flowers, scrub and trees, making it a great walking route and a hidden treasure for bird watchers. Small Tortoiseshell and Red Admiral butterflies can also often be spotted during the summer and look out for flowers like Shepherd's Purse, whose seed purses are said to resemble the pouches that medieval peasants wore on their belts.

Along the one-and-a-half-mile walk, lots of old railway tunnels and bridges can still be seen. The Dundee to Newtyle railway was one of the first passenger trains in Scotland and the first commercial railway in northern Scotland. It was created as a link between the bustling hub of manufacturing that was Dundee and the valley of Strathmore, however it terminated at Newtyle, a small village situated eleven miles north west of Dundee. The line was opened in 1831 and by 1833 it was home to the first steam locomotives in the country. It remained in operation until the 1960s when it was closed down as part of the infamous Dr Beeching cuts.

In its own way, the railway was one of the most important early lines in Scotland. It was the first not to rely on a coalfield for the bulk of its traffic and was built to connect the farming areas of Dundee to the harbour, carrying general traffic in both directions.

The main entrances to The Miley can be found on Old King's Cross Road and on Clepington Road and are easily identifiable by their wrought-iron gates.

The award-winning Dundee Miley Group looks after the Reserve, collecting litter and raising money for the management and upkeep of the area.

10. Camperdown Mansion House and Park

Camperdown mansion house is described as one of the finest Neoclassical homes in Britain, and the largest remaining Greek Revival house in Scotland. It is located in the grounds of Camperdown Park, a 400-acre public park situated four miles north west of the city centre.

The estate of Camperdown was originally known as Lundie. Bought by Alexander Duncan in 1682, a sixteenth-century house existed on the estate. In 1797, during the French revolutionary wars, one member of the Duncan family, Admiral Adam Duncan (1731–1804) encountered the Dutch fleet off the coast near a village called Camperdown. The ensuing battle lasted five hours and the Dutch surrendered to Admiral Duncan on board his ship, the *Venerable*. This victory made Duncan a hero and he was rewarded by being raised to the peerage of Viscount Duncan of Camperdown. A statue commemorating Admiral Duncan can be seen in the city centre outside St Paul's Cathedral.

In 1820, Admiral Duncan's son and heir, Robert, the 1st Earl of Camperdown, commissioned the building of a new house, designed by leading Edinburgh architect William Burn. The original house was demolished and the existing mansion was built between 1824 and 1828. The Earl of Camperdown renamed the estate and mansion Camperdown, in honour of his father's victory.

The mansion house was built using white sandstone which came from Cullalo, on the north shore of the Firth of Forth. The exterior features a six-column wide portico in true Greek Revival style. The interior boasts interconnecting staterooms and a double-height central hall that is roofed and lit with a stained-glass dome, which details Admiral Duncan's Coat of Arms and his gold medal in the centre.

The green open spaces surrounding the mansion were designed and laid out by Admiral Duncan. During your visit, take a moment to marvel at over 190 species of trees that can be found in the park.

Camperdown is noted for being the origin of the unique Camperdown Elm. The official name for the elm is *Ulmus glabra Camperdownii* and it is a short, broad, weeping variety of elm. It was discovered in 1835 by the estate's forester when he found a contorted Wych Elm (*Ulmus glabra*) branch on the ground. He then produced the first Camperdown Elm by grafting it to the trunk of a normal Wych Elm. From that day, every Camperdown Elm has been produced from a cutting taken from that original tree. Today, the original Camperdown Elm is still thriving in Camperdown Park and is known as the Admiral's Tree.

The estate remained the seat of the Duncan's for three generations, after which the house was inherited by a cousin who became the last occupant. It was then purchased by the local council in 1946 after its

contents were sold at a four-day auction.

Today, the mansion house is used for special events and can be visited on selected open days throughout the year.

The estate was officially opened to the public as Camperdown Country Park in 1949 and today is Dundee's largest park. It offers a wide range of activities for all the family to enjoy, including an 18-hole golf course, the Camperdown Wildlife Centre, a pirate-themed adventure playground, a duck pond and woodland trails. The park is also used to host events such as the Easter Fun Day, the Dundee Flower and Food Festival in September and the ever-popular 'Meet Santa' event at Christmas.

WEST DUNDEE

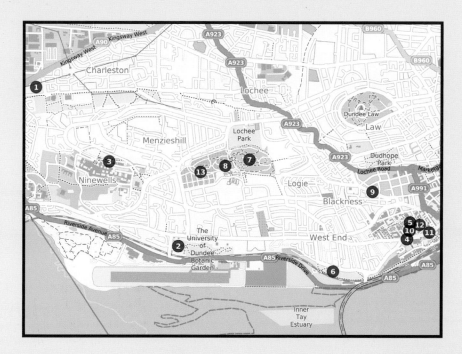

1. Dundee's Stonehenge
2. The Macro Micro Studio and The Botanic Garden
3. Thomas John MacLagan: Pioneer in the Development of Aspirin
4. Legendary *Lemmings*
5. Williamina Fleming: Women and Astronomy
6. Magdalen Green Bandstand
7. Britain's First Purpose-Built Public Observatory
8. Balgay Park
9. The White Ladies
10. Geddes Quadrangle
11. Frances Wright: The World's First Feminist
12. The D'Arcy Thompson Zoology Museum
13. James Bowman Lindsay: Let There Be Light!

1. Dundee's Stonehenge

In an area to the north west of Dundee, known as Charleston, there lies an ancient monument called Balgarthno Stone Circle. The site consists of a recumbent stone circle, approximately 23 feet in diameter, with one non-recumbent stone. All of the nine original boulders are still in place today, although all are somewhat weathered.

Stone circles were built in many parts of Britain around 4,500–5,300 years ago, between the Neolithic and the Bronze Age, and Dundee's stones are one such example.

The stones are said to reveal an affinity with the movement of the sun and the moon and are considered to be ritual monuments where local Pictish people met to commemorate the dead. Most of the stones feature symbols, shapes, objects and animals which were carved by Pictish craftsmen into natural boulders. Later stones were shaped into crosses and feature Pictish symbols next to Christian motifs as well as scenes of battle and hunting.

It is thought that the meanings and uses of the stones changed over time and adapted according to the needs of the communities that surrounded them. Stones are the most identifiable objects associated with the culture of the Picts and although historians the world over have tried to understand what the symbols mean, they remain a mystery. This is largely because there are no surviving Pictish writings, and accounts of Pictish people are scarce.

Balgarthno Stone Circle was known as the 'Farm of Corn': the fields surrounding the stones have been farmed for hundreds of years. The name Balgarthno means Garthnait's Farm. Garthnait is a Pictish name that was adopted by Gaelic speakers in medieval times.

The stones are believed to have played a key role in

the life of the area's early residents. Today the stone circle is known locally as the Myrekirk as the stones are located next to Myrekirk Road.

Artefacts from stone circles are scarce. An excavation of Balgarthno circle in the mid-twentieth century however, uncovered some jet fragments and flint from the late prehistoric period, which confirmed the antiquity of the site. They are now housed in the National Museum of Scotland in Edinburgh.

2. The Macro Micro Studio and The Botanic Garden

Located in the city's Botanic Garden, the Macro Micro Studio is a self-sufficient building prototype which will be entirely powered by renewable energy. It was designed and constructed by a team of staff and students from the departments of Architecture & Planning and Physics & Engineering at the University of Dundee.

The project focuses on integrated, sustainable energy solutions and the way in which they can be used to develop affordable, low-energy housing across Scotland. In doing so the studio, and its associated projects, aim to help local businesses become regional and national leaders in low-carbon design and solutions.

Of course, this is not the only hidden gem that lurks in the Botanic Garden. Located in 23 acres of south-facing land, the Garden features a wide range of indigenous British plants and representative collections of imported plants from all continents of the world. It boasts fine examples of conifers and broad-leaved trees and shrubs, a water garden, tropical and temperate glasshouses, a herb garden and a visitor centre.

The Botanic Garden opened in 1971 and is home to 43 per cent of the world's pine species and 52 per cent of the world's conifer genera – little-known facts to many.

Look out for the arched well that was designed and built by Edward Kemp, the first curator of the Garden. The water in this area is very pure and has a high magnesium content. On emerging, it has a minimum temperature of 3.5°C which allows climatically marginal plants to be grown in the ornamental pool.

The glasshouses offer noteworthy collections of tropical and temperate plants including conifers from Asia, the Mediterranean, North Africa and Australasia,

as well as plants from Brazil, all of which are normally unable to survive in Scotland.

Something else to admire in the Garden is the outstanding maze of drystane dykes (the Scottish term for drystone walls) in the Garden of Evolution. Uniquely, these walls surround examples of plants that together have evolved over a period of 1,200 million years.

The Garden is also home to an award-winning visitor centre which hosts a range of exhibitions throughout the year.

The founding principles of the Garden are science, education and conservation and its overarching aim is to conserve and protect threatened species of plants and to bring these to the attention of the community.

The Garden is open all year round and offers visitors the chance to enjoy a glimpse of paradise not so far from the madding crowd.

3. Thomas John MacLagan: Pioneer in the Development of Aspirin

Number 136 Nethergate in Dundee was home to a man whose legacy lives on all over the world.

His name was Dr Thomas John MacLagan (1838–1903). Originally from Scone, he qualified from the Edinburgh Medical School in 1860 and became Resident Medical Superintendent of the former Dundee Royal Infirmary. There, MacLagan made some significant changes, including introducing an improved diet for hospital patients and promoting the use of medicinal wine which reduced hospital mortality in Dundee to one of the lowest levels in Scotland.

During his work he became the first doctor in the country to actively use the clinical thermometer, an instrument that up until then had never been taken seriously in medical circles.

In 1866, once the fever epidemic that had ravaged Dundee for two years had passed, MacLagan decided to venture into general practice. He set up his surgical

rooms in the Nethergate where he was inundated with patients suffering from acute or chronic rheumatism. Soon, he devoted his time to finding a treatment for the condition that plagued so much of Dundee's population.

It was in these surgical rooms that Dr Thomas MacLagan discovered, studied and trialled what would come to be known as aspirin – one of the most important drugs in history and one of the most widely used pharmaceutical products in the world today.

MacLagan was convinced that the willow tree held the cure. In 1874, he used salicin, the bitter principle contained within the bark of the white willow tree, to carry out a trial on eight of his patients who suffered from rheumatism.

Within forty-eight hours, there was a marked improvement in the patients' symptoms. He carried out further trials and in 1876, he published his findings that highlighted the benefits of salicin for the treatment of acute or chronic rheumatism.

His studies were read worldwide and because of them, alongside investigations in Germany, acetyl-salicylic acid, otherwise known as aspirin, was created. Twenty years later the German scientist Felix Hoffman discovered a process to produce the acid synthetically and gave the drug its brand name.

At the time of MacLagan's death in 1903, it was said that, 'he deserves a niche in the Temple of Fame as one of the great benefactors of the human race.'

MacLagan's original microscope is held in the Tayside Medical History Museum. Based at Ninewells Hospital & Medical School, the Museum's collections showcase the extraordinary history of pioneering medical research and practice in Dundee and the surrounding region, and are among the finest in Scotland.

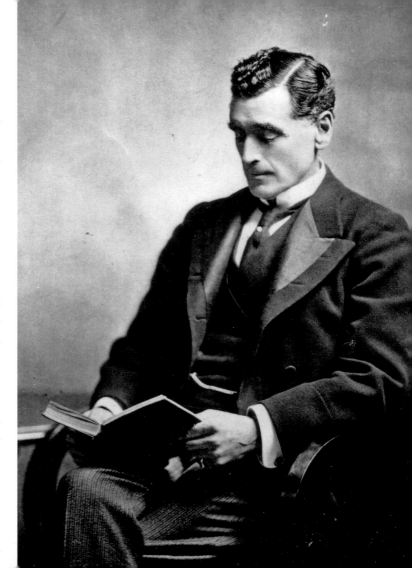

4. Legendary *Lemmings*

One of the UK's first ever blockbuster video games titles was created in Dundee, selling 55,000 copies on its first day of release and recording a total of over 15 million sales worldwide.

Lemmings was the brainchild of Dundee-based company DMA Design and was released for play on the Amiga games console in 1991. To win the puzzle-platformer game, players had to assign abilities to the rodents in order to guide them through an exit while avoiding traps and obstacles. Its easy-to-play yet challenging-to-beat concept quickly made it a global success, gaining critical acclaim.

Such was the game's popularity that it was adapted for play on thirty-one different systems. It gave way to six sequels including *Xmas Lemmings, Oh No! More Lemmings*, and *Lemmings 2: The Tribes,* along with two spin-offs, namely *Lemmings Paintball* and the PlayStation game, *The Adventures Of Lomax*.

Thanks to the success of *Lemmings*, DMA Design became a pioneer in the games industry and in 1997, it released the even more successful, *Grand Theft Auto*. This game and its sequel put DMA Design on the world map as a leader in its field and the company moved to Edinburgh and rebranded as Rockstar North.

In 2014, the legendary lemmings were immortalised in bronze as part of Dundee's public art programme. Today, visitors can spot three lemmings climbing over a stone pillar on the Perth Road opposite Airlie Place, just a few steps away from where the game was created.

Sculptor Alyson Conway created the bronze masterpiece to celebrate the fact that the game was produced in Dundee and to acknowledge the impact the series has had on the Scottish games industry. She chose the location to give the impression that the lemmings had wandered out of their birthplace at DMA Design's original studio and walked along to their current location where they now welcome people to Dundee's Digital Media Park.

The low stone wall and pillars represent a 2D game level which the Lemmings are trying to cross – a lookout stands on top of the pillar and behind him there is a climber making his way up, while below there is a builder laying bricks.

The sculpture however, remains unfinished – the original proposal incorporated seven lemmings but funding was only initially available for three of the furry creatures. It is hoped that extra funding will become available in the future so that more lemmings can join the hard-working army.

5. Williamina Fleming: Women and Astronomy

Williamina Paton Stevens Fleming (1857–1911) was born at 86 Nethergate in Dundee and went on to become Harvard University's Curator of Astronomical Photographs, discovering hundreds of stars and charting one of the first maps of the skies.

When she was twenty-one, after having been educated in Dundee and teaching in its public schools since the age of fourteen, she moved to Boston with her husband James Orr Fleming. The couple had a son. However, Fleming's husband abandoned her and she was forced to find work to support her new baby.

Rather fortuitously, she became a housekeeper for Professor Edward Charles Pickering. He was a Professor of Astronomy at Harvard and the director of the Harvard College Observatory, and was becoming frustrated by the poor work of his male assistants. Noting the skill and intellect that Fleming displayed, he decided to employ her to do clerical work and mathematical calculations at the Observatory.

It soon became clear that Fleming had a natural talent for astronomy and she created a system of classifying stars according to how much hydrogen they displayed in their spectra – the unique pattern of lines caused by the refraction of a star's light through a prism. This new system became known as the 'Pickering–Fleming System' and over the next nine years, Fleming catalogued more than 10,000 stars. In fact, throughout her career, she discovered 59 gaseous nebulae, 310 variable stars and 10 novae, and discovered the Horsehead Nebula in 1888 on a photographic plate – an incredible feat for someone without a formal education in astronomy. She published her findings in 1890 in the *Henry Draper Catalogue of Stellar Spectra*.

In 1898, Fleming became Curator of Astronomical Photographs at Harvard College Observatory, making

her the first woman ever to hold this position. In 1906, she was made an honorary member of the Royal Astronomical Society of London. Soon after, she was appointed as honorary fellow in astronomy at Wellesley College.

In 1907 Fleming published *A Photographic Study of Variable Stars* and she reached the pinnacle of her career in 1910 when she discovered white dwarfs – hot dense stars that are white in colour. In 1911, Fleming published *Spectra and Photographic Magnitudes of Stars in Standard Regions*.

She died of pneumonia in 1911 at the age of fifty-four, in Boston. Shortly before her death, she was awarded the Guadalupe Almendaro medal by the Astronomical Society of Mexico for her discovery of new stars. Today, the lunar crater 'Fleming' is named jointly after her and Alexander Fleming.

6. Magdalen Green Bandstand

Built in 1890 and listed in 1986, the ornate Magdalen Green Bandstand is one of Dundee's lesser-known landmarks.

It was built at the Saracen Foundry by Walter Macfarlane & Co., of Glasgow and is located in Magdalen Green Park in the city's west end.

The bandstand was immortalised in the paintings of one of Scotland's most celebrated artists, Dundonian, James McIntosh Patrick (1907–1998).

In fact it was proceeds from the auctioning of one of his watercolours, combined with public and local authority donations in 1988, that enabled the resurrection of the bandstand after it had fallen into disrepair.

The bandstand was again extensively restored in 1990 and in 2009 some minor repairs were carried out.

Magdalen Green itself is Dundee's oldest city park and has been in use for some 400 years. It was created in its current form in the 1840s under the direction of Provost Alexander Lawson with the aim of bolstering employment during a slump in the town. Today it is a firm favourite with sunworshippers, dog walkers and sports enthusiasts alike.

In 2010, Magdalen Green became an integral part of Dundee's flood defences. Four large water tanks were installed to hold excess rainwater during periods of high tide.

The volunteer community group, The 'Friends of Magdalen Green', works to protect and enhance the Green and the bandstand for the benefit of present and future generations.

Today, the bandstand is home to performances by brass bands on Sunday afternoons during the summer months and occasionally hosts weddings. In early June the annual festival 'Westfest' takes place on the Green. This community-organised event is Dundee's largest open-air concert.

Why not while away the hours at Magdalen Green the next time you're in Dundee?

7. Britain's First Purpose-Built Public Observatory

Dundee's Mills Observatory was gifted by bequest in 1935 from John Mills, the linen and twine manufacturer. He was a keen astronomer and had an observatory on the Law during the nineteenth century but wanted to ensure that the citizens of Dundee could look up and marvel at the wonders of the solar system. As such, the Mills Observatory was the first observatory in Britain, and second in the world, to be built for the sole purpose of encouraging public understanding of science.

The Observatory is located at the summit of Balgay Hill. It is built of sandstone and features a distinctive dome which is 22 feet in diameter. The dome is one of only two made from papier-mâché to survive in the United Kingdom; the other is located at the Godlee Observatory in Manchester.

The dome houses the 10-inch (250mm) Cooke refracting telescope that was built by Thomas Cooke

of York in 1871. Due to its age and size, it is now only occasionally used under careful supervision.

The main telescope in the Observatory is a 16-inch (400mm) Dobsonian reflector which provides outstanding views of the Moon, other planets and deep space objects. When the Observatory first opened it housed an 18-inch (450mm) reflecting telescope which can still be seen today in the display area.

There is also a fully computerised 12-inch (300mm) Meade Schmidt Cassegrain reflector telescope that can automatically find 30,000 objects in the sky. This telescope allows viewers to safely observe the sun during the summer months.

From October to March, the planetarium shows, with assistance from members of the Dundee Astronomical Society, offer visitors the chance to learn about constellations, planets and other jewels of the

night sky. There are also regular displays about the solar system and space exploration.

From April to September, the Observatory is open on selected dates when visitors can take part in a programme of events including family workshops, talks and solar viewings. Admission to this wonder is free for all to enjoy, so why not take a trip to the stars on your next visit to Dundee?

8. Balgay Park

Opened in 1871 by the Earl of Dalhousie, Balgay Park is a beautiful public park and cemetery that retains much of its original layout.

Not to be missed is the picturesque, category B listed 80-feet span footbridge that reaches across a natural rock gorge. The decorative cast-iron crossing was constructed in 1877 and the height from roadway to the bottom of the parapet is 40 feet. It was originally built to allow people to cross from one side of the park to the other without having to tackle the steep ravines that separated the two.

The bridge is said to have been designed by George Hird of the local authority's engineering department. It features cast iron interlaced railings with floral finials and a central inscription plaque that bears the town's arms.

In the eighteenth and nineteenth centuries, the avenue which separates Balgay Park from the neighbouring cemetery was known as 'The Windy Glack'. It was so-called due to its location, as it acted as a tunnel for the winds that came off of the Sidlaw Hills – a range of hills of volcanic origin that lie a few miles north of Dundee. Up until 1830, the Windy Glack was used by smugglers as Balgay Hill was once a meeting point for criminals who frequented the area with illegal alcohol.

Today the park offers a children's play area, a rose-garden, a bandstand and tennis courts. Don't forget to make your way to the highest point of the park, Balgay Hill, to take in splendid views of the city and to visit Mills Observatory, the first purpose-built public observatory in Britain.

9. The White Ladies

No city is complete without frightful tales of its very own White Lady. Dundee is said to be home to at least three white ladies, all named after the white period costume they are said to wear.

The White Lady o' Balgay Bridge is thought to roam the cast-iron Victorian footbridge that stretches over the ravine in Balgay Park. The Bridge connects Balgay Hill to the footpaths of Balgay Cemetery. There are endless different reports of sightings of this Lady who has become engrained in Dundee's folklore. Some say she runs crying from the bridge into the cemetery and that she can be summoned at midnight by walking across the bridge three times. Other more gruesome tales purport that she can be seen reading a letter then bursting into tears before jumping off the bridge, or that she can turn those who unknowingly summon her into a pool of blood, and that she can even push unsuspecting bystanders off the bridge.

The White Lady of the Coffin Mill is said to live in a former jute mill that is located on Brook Street. She is believed to be the spirit of a mill girl who died when her long hair became trapped in a loom, crushing her to death. According to hearsay, she can most often be seen pacing the enclosed exterior bridge that connected the two parts of the mill, known as the Coffin Mill.

This mill was the south range of Logie Works, Dundee's first big textiles factory which was built in 1828. It was expanded in later years to become the largest flax works of the nineteenth century from 1842 to 1865. Where the name the Coffin Mill came from remains unclear. However, it is most likely explained by the coffin-shaped interior courtyard that is enclosed by the former mill which has now been converted into flats.

A similar white lady is said to haunt Dundee's jute

museum, Verdant Works. A former mill, it is located on West Henderson's Wynd. The story goes that a white lady can be seen walking across the bridge that connects the two parts of the complex and is visible from the gateway entrance.

Some say that the White Lady of the Coffin Mill and the White Lady of the jute museum are in fact the same ghost. Others maintain that the source of the museum's apparition is the spirit of a girl who was employed in the mill and who became tangled in a carding machine and died before she could be released.

Whatever white lady you believe in, it's clear that Dundee has its fair share of ghastly ghouls!

10. Geddes Quadrangle

Geddes Quadrangle is one of the most beautiful places on the campus of the University of Dundee.

The Quadrangle was completed in 1912. It is named after Professor Patrick Geddes (1854–1932), the biologist, sociologist, educationalist and town planner who taught botany at University College Dundee between 1889 and 1914.

He transformed the space into a teaching garden. Each bed was planted as a specific scientific group. Geddes believed that all learning should be based on real life experience and, in fact, plans for a Botanic Garden in Dundee were first advanced by Professor Geddes in 1906. His plans were never realised but the University's Botanic Garden eventually opened to the public in 1971.

An oasis of calm, the Quadrangle boasts manicured lawns and a bronze sundial mounted on a grand three-tier plinth takes pride of place in the centre. The sundial is inscribed with the words 'British Association 1912', commemorating the meeting in Dundee that year of the British Association for the Advancement of Science.

The Quadrange is also home to some of the University's finest old buildings including the Carnegie Building (Centre for Energy, Petroleum and Mineral Law Policy), the Harris Building (Electronic Engineering and Physics) and the Peters Building (Centre for Water Law, Policy and Science).

The secluded corner can be accessed via Small's Wynd. It is an ideal spot for a picnic and is a haven of tranquillity amidst the hustle and bustle of city life. To the south there is a sunken garden with a large *Eucalyptus gunnii* tree planted with Thyme, Euonymus, Mahonia and Fuschia. Why not take a moment to soak up the atmosphere here during your visit to Dundee?

11. Frances Wright: The World's First Feminist

Frances Wright, (1795–1852) was a feminist, social reformer and freethinker. She was born in Dundee and lived in the Nethergate area of the city.

At the age of two, Wright and her sister were orphaned and moved to England to live with their aunt. There, Wright was taught ideas founded on the philosophy of French materialists.

However, as a young woman, Wright returned to Scotland to stay with her great-uncle, a professor of philosophy at Glasgow College. She spent her winters studying and her summers visiting the Scottish Highlands. Her first book, *A Few Days in Athens*, was published in 1822 and looked at materialistic philosophy. Soon after this, she and her sister travelled to the United States where her play *Altorf*, about Swiss independence, was produced in New York City.

Wright believed in feminism and in universal equality. She was firmly opposed to organised religion, greed and capitalism. As part of this, she demanded that the government provided free public education for all children over two-years-of-age in state-supported boarding schools, and she fought for women's rights to use birth control and for their sexual freedom.

Her work and actions in America were based on the teachings of the French utopian socialist, Charles Fourier, who believed that the progress of civilisation depended on the progress of women.

In 1825 Wright published *A Plan for the Gradual Abolition of Slavery in the United States Without Danger of Loss to the Citizens of the South*. This work proposed that a colony should be started outside the United States to educate and emancipate slaves and it urged Congress to set aside tracts of land for this purpose.

Wright then purchased a 640-acre piece of land in Tennessee and called it the Nashoba Commune.

There, she aimed to build a self-sustaining multi-racial community. She bought slaves, located them in Nashoba and promised them freedom. However, things didn't work out as planned and scandal emerged over claims of inter-racial marriage, which damaged financial support for the settlement. The colony never recovered. Eventually, Wright left the community for Dale Owen's socialist community in Indiana and in 1830 she returned to Nashoba to arrange for the emancipation of the slaves and their colonisation in Haiti.

In 1829, Wright and Owen co-founded the radical *Free Inquirer* newspaper in New York City and Wright wrote the *Views of Society and Manners in America*. Through their writing, Owen and Wright led the free-thinking movement, calling for liberalised divorce laws, birth-control, free secular education run by the state, and the political organisation of the working classes.

Their work was so popular and controversial that it was translated into several languages and was read throughout the United States and Europe.

Defying convention at the time, Wright gave a series of lectures that attacked religion, authoritarian education and politics and defended equal rights for women, calling for legal marriage to be replaced by a union which was based on moral obligation.

In 1831, Wright married and lived in Paris until 1835 when she settled in Cincinnati. As an activist in the American Popular Health Movement between 1830 and 1840, she fought for women to be involved in health and medicine.

Wright divorced in 1850, became a US citizen in 1852 and died the same year as a result of a fall on an icy staircase. This remarkable Dundonian is buried in the Spring Grove Cemetery in Cincinnati.

12. The D'Arcy Thompson Zoology Museum

Hidden in the Carnelley Building of The University of Dundee is the fascinating D'Arcy Thompson Zoology Museum. It offers a unique insight into the work of the celebrated polymath, Sir D'Arcy Wentworth Thompson (1860–1948).

A leading Scottish mathematical biologist and Classics scholar, Sir D'Arcy Thompson is best remembered for his influential 1917 work *On Growth and Form*. It was this book that, for the first time, identified and explained morphogenesis – the process that causes plants and animals to develop their shape. Since then, his studies have been an inspiration to pioneering biologists, mathematicians and even artists.

Sir D'Arcy Thompson went on to publish around 300 works during his career and was one of Dundee's most illustrious residents. In 1885 he took up the first Chair of Biology at what was then known as the University College Dundee. Eccentric by nature, he became a well-known figure throughout the city and actively participated in local organisations including the Dundee Working Men's Field Club, the Dundee Social Union and the Dundee Naturalists Society. He was strongly in favour of education and improvements for all in Dundee.

Importantly, during his thirty-two years in the city, Sir D'Arcy Thompson also established a large zoology museum for teaching and research at the University of Dundee, collecting specimens from all over the world. At the time, the Museum was one of the largest of its kind in the country, and specialised in Arctic zoology.

It was this collection of specimens that provided the bedrock for his research into the mathematical principles of nature and resulted in the publication of his pioneering book.

With unreserved commitment, Sir D'Arcy Thompson collected hundreds of spirit specimens and over 200 skeletons in preparation in the first few years alone – many hundreds more followed. By befriending the Dundee whaling skippers, he was able to encourage them to bring back specimens for him from the Arctic. He also purchased specimens from dealers in London, negotiated duplicates from other museums, such as the British Museum in London, and bought a skeleton of an elephant from the Dublin Zoological Gardens.

Sir D'Arcy Thompson's original Museum was demolished in the 1950s and his collection was dispersed – only important teaching material was retained. Many specimens were donated to the Royal Scottish Museum in Edinburgh; others to the British Museum of Natural History. A complete catalogue of the original Museum has never been found, so the full scale of Sir D'Arcy Thompson's collection will never be known.

However, a new version of the Museum was opened in 2008, housing many of the polymath's original specimens. The D'Arcy Thompson Zoology Museum is located in Park Place and is open regularly to the public on Friday afternoons during the University's summer break, and for special events throughout the year. It features an outstanding variety of mammals, birds, fish, reptiles and insects from all over the world, as well as some of Thompson's original models and teaching charts.

Meanwhile, the Tower Foyer & Lamb Galleries at the University of Dundee stage regular free public exhibitions based on the University's collections as well as on loans from other institutions and private collections.

Sir D'Arcy Thompson was elected as Fellow of the Royal Society of London for Improving Natural Knowledge in 1916 and was Vice President of the Society from 1931 to 1933. In 1937 he was knighted, and in 1942 he was awarded the Daniel Giraud Elliot Medal from the National Academy of Sciences. In 1946 he was presented with the Darwin Medal.

He left Dundee in 1917 to take up his appointment as Chair of Natural History at the University of St Andrews.

13. James Bowman Lindsay: Let There Be Light!

James Bowman Lindsay (1799–1862) was an inventor, astronomer, philologist and author who is credited with early developments in a number of areas, most famously incandescent lighting and telegraphy. Born in Arbroath, he was educated at the University of St Andrews and lectured in science and mathematics at what is now the University of Abertay, Dundee.

It is widely acknowledged that in 1835, Lindsay demonstrated a constant electric light at a public meeting in Dundee and thereby developed the first prototype of an incandescent lamp. His concern with electric light was based on the need to provide a safe method of lighting for Dundee's jute mills where fires caused by candles had devastated the lives of many workers.

He is believed to have said that by using the light that he produced he was able to read a book at a distance of one-and-a-half-feet. However, his claims are not well documented and he did little to establish his findings. Having progressed the electric light to his own satisfaction, he did not develop the lighting device any further. As a result, it was Thomas Edison who was officially recognised for the invention of the incandescent light bulb over forty years later.

Once he had developed the electric light, Lindsay then moved onto the area of arc welding and made the then revolutionary suggestion of using electric arc welding to join cables and using anodes to prevent corrosion. He knew of the difficulties of laying transatlantic cable and wanted to solve them. However, his ideas did not see widespread application until many years later.

In 1843, Lindsay came up with the idea of laying a telegraph wire under the sea floor across the Atlantic. By 1853, after years of experimentation throughout the country, Lindsay was able to demonstrate transmission of a message across two miles of water by using insulated wires. He then experimented without wires and patented his system. Again, he did not develop his findings and his device was found to be flawed.

A deeply humane man, Lindsay's real achievements lay in his vision and creativity as he lacked the ruthlessness to promote his innovations. His 'Lecture on Electricity' in Dundee in 1836 and 1837 effectively foretold the development of the information society and he predicted cities lit by electricity.

As a philologist, his achievements were equally significant and in 1828, he began work on the compilation of a dictionary in fifty languages which went on for more than a quarter of a century but was sadly not completed before his death.

In 1858, Prime Minister Lord Derby granted Lindsay a pension of £100 a year on the recommendation of Queen Victoria.

Lindsay died in 1862 and was buried in the Western Cemetery in Dundee. Thanks to public subscription in 1901, a marble monument was erected at his grave in recognition of his achievements and contributions to society.

EAST DUNDEE

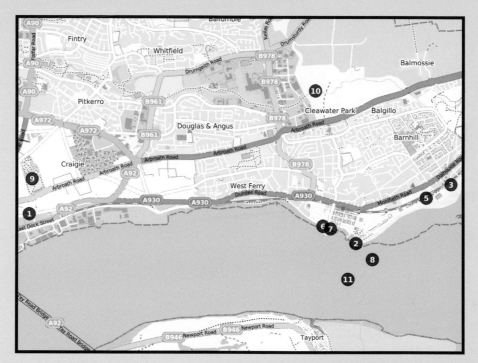

1. Frankenstein in Dundee

2. The Broughty Ferry Castle Guns

3. The Barnhill Rock Garden

4. Patrick Blair: The First Doctor in Britain to Dissect an Elephant

5. The Broughty Ferry Nature Reserve

6. The Fisherman's Graveyard

7. The Broughty Ferry Life Boat Disaster

8. Dolphin Watching

9. Baxter Park

10. Dundee's Grand Canyon

11. General Monck's Treasure

1. Frankenstein in Dundee

Frankenstein lives on in Dundee! Or at least the memory of the cottage mentioned in the book does. Have a look at the commemorative plaque on South Baffin Street which states that on that very site stood the cottage which was mentioned in Mary Wollstonecraft Godwin's classic gothic novel, *Frankenstein*.

The connection between Dundee and *Frankenstein* dates back to 1812 when Mary Godwin, later known as Mary Shelley, was sent to the city as a child by her father to stay with his friend William Baxter. It is said that Mary endured a strained relationship with her stepmother but idealised her own mother who had sadly passed away shortly after Mary's birth. Alongside this, Mary suffered ill health and it was advised that she should seek respite away from London.

Mary set sail for Dundee in 1812 and during her time in the city she lived at the Baxter's home known as 'The Cottage'. This was a stately home, located where South Baffin Street now stands and was originally built as the Countess of Strathmore's dower house. There, she became close friends with the Baxters' daughters Isabel and Christina. As a close-knit family, the Baxters showed Mary a different kind of life to the one she had always known – a family life based on mutual dependence, affection, harmony and respect. She came to regard the Baxters as a source of emotional support and they are said to have provided the basis for her fictional representations of the nuclear family.

As well as this, the beach and hills around Dundee were believed to have sparked Mary's imagination and she later used them to describe scenery in her writing.

Mary returned to London in May 1814 but it wasn't until 1818 that *Frankenstein* was published. There are elements in *Frankenstein* that could be interpreted as having been written as a result of her experiences in

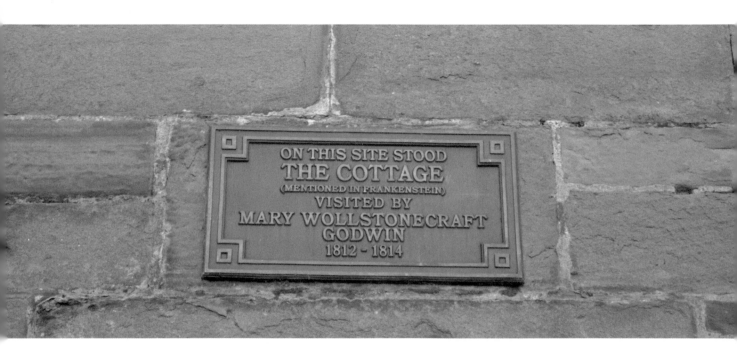

Dundee. For example, her account of the relationship between technology and people was perhaps founded on the first-hand experience of jute production that Mary would have acquired while staying with the Baxter family.

It is impossible to say how much of an impact Mary's time in Dundee had on her writing but it did serve as a broadening influence and, as she stated herself, gave her the space she needed for her imagination to develop.

2. The Broughty Ferry Castle Guns

Remarkably, the three guns that can now be seen in the grounds of Broughty Ferry Castle were, up until not so long ago, used as bollards on Broughty Ferry pier. It wasn't until a savvy visitor spotted them in 1989, that it became apparent they were in fact rare surviving examples of Armstrong Guns.

In 1990, the guns were removed from the pier – each had been partially buried within the concrete of the pier and all were badly corroded. The guns were then renovated before being put on display in the Castle along with modern copies of the carriages which would originally have been used to support them.

They were identified as Rifled Breech-Loaders, designed by Sir William Armstrong and made between 1859 and 1866. Two of the guns are 40-pounders of 35 hundredweight each and the other is a 40-pounder of 32 hundredweight. The guns were so-called because they fired a 40-pound shot. They were relatively common during their time, however very few have survived: three in Jersey and one in Bermuda. None were known to have existed in the United Kingdom until the Broughty Ferry visitor's serendipitous discovery.

Further research suggests that the guns would originally have been installed in Broughty Ferry Castle when it was rebuilt in the mid-nineteenth century. Other guns would also have been housed in the Castle when it was re-modelled, including five 10-inch guns and two 68-pounders. The ammunition for these guns was kept in a magazine that was constructed in the ground floor of the tower house. This hidden underground gem gives an insight into what life must have been like for soldiers who were based there. The magazine is open to the public on selected dates throughout the year.

Often called the 'romantic ruin', Broughty Ferry Castle is located on a strategically important rock promontory at the mouth of the River Tay. It protected the entrance to the Tay Estuary and originally it could only be reached by a causeway at low tide. The site is believed to have been first fortified in 1454 when the fourth Earl of Angus was given permission to build there.

The Castle faced many sieges throughout its history and marks made by cannon shot can still be seen on its walls. It was held by the English for two years before being taken back by the Protestant Scots faction. The eighteenth century saw the Castle degrade to an abandoned ruin and at the end of the Crimean war in 1855, it was purchased by the War Office as an outpost to control the Tay and defend it against possible invasion by the Russians. In 1860, when war with France was thought to be impending, it was deemed necessary to refortify the site.

However, as war became more sophisticated, the position of the Castle proved to be its downfall and it was labelled 'badly built, badly designed and utterly useless for the purpose for which it was constructed.'

Today, the Castle operates as a museum. It showcases the history of Broughty Ferry and its people, environment and wildlife.

It also features the Orchar Gallery that contains around twenty-four oil paintings from the James Guthrie Orchar Collection which, with over 300 paintings in total, is recognised as one of the most important collections of Scottish Victorian art in the country. James Guthrie Orchar (1825–1898), was one of Dundee's most distinguished businessmen and a former Provost of Broughty Ferry. On his death, he gifted his extensive private art collection to be displayed in the town.

To the north-east of the Castle is a two-storey building that was once the depot of the Broughty Castle Submarine Miners. The depot was built in the

1880s and the volunteer Tay Division Submarine Miners was set up in 1888.

In the event of war, the miners planned to lay explosive mines across the Tay to prevent enemy naval attacks. There were two steam boats that laid and retrieved mines. Similar units were based in Greenock, Leith and across the British Empire in Malta, Hong Kong, Canada and Bermuda. The Miners remained at the Castle depot, which was said to be one of the best equipped and most complete in the country, until 1907.

Entrance to Broughty Ferry Castle is free so that all visitors and locals can learn about its history and culture.

3. The Barnhill Rock Garden

The Barnhill Rock Garden is a beautiful oasis tucked away in the corner of Broughty Ferry, at the east end of the waterfront area, known as the Esplanade.

It provides a wonderful open space for all to enjoy and extends to more than five acres. With a wide array of plants and shrubs, as well as ponds, springs, wildlife and panoramic views out over the River Tay, the Garden has been a firm favourite with many generations of locals over the years.

It is situated on a former nine-hole golf course, which was constructed on the advice of legendary golfer, Tom Morris Senior. The course was laid out in 1895 when the Dundee to Aberdeen railway line was built and was completed in 1896 at a total cost of £80.

The Garden itself began life in 1955. An area of volcanic rock, which at one point had been the old shoreline, was cleared and over time it was extended eastwards across areas that had once been sand dunes. There were originally five natural springs and although most dried up in 1976, one remains today – the lowest pond on the site.

Just along from this pond, in the woodland area, is the unique Geddes Glasshouse that was gifted to the Friends of Barnhill Rock Garden. The Glasshouse opened in 2007 and has been developed as a multi-purpose building that offers visitors an attractive and informative interpretation point. The Glasshouse also hosts a wide variety of community events including children's programmes, poetry readings, art classes and environmental initiatives.

The Friends of the Barnhill Rock Garden work hard to ensure the future of the garden's long-established collection of plant material from all corners of the world. They carry out gardening activities and give generously of their time to allow people to enjoy the surroundings.

The Barnhill Rock Garden is open to the public all year round. Entrance is free so that all visitors can relax and take time to get close to nature during their trip to Broughty Ferry.

4. Patrick Blair: The First Doctor in Britain to Dissect an Elephant

In 1706, a travelling Indian elephant that was on exhibit around the North of Scotland, collapsed and died just outside Broughty Ferry.

While locals tried to claim parts of the animal as memorabilia, the distinguished Dundee physician, Dr Patrick Blair (1680–1728), was given permission to carry out a dissection of the carcass. In doing so, he became the first doctor in Britain to dissect an elephant and to complete a pioneering scientific study of the animal's internal organs and skeleton.

Local butchers assisted Dr Blair with the dissection and the elephant's bones were recovered and mounted. They were then placed on exhibit in Dundee and the animal's skin was stuffed. In 1710, Blair published his findings in a journal entitled *Philosophical Transactions of the Royal Society of London*. In 1712, the Royal Society elected Blair as a Fellow and in the same year, King's College awarded him a Doctor of Medicine. A year later, his work on the elephant was produced as a pamphlet called *Osteographia Elephantina*.

Dr Patrick Blair was born in Lethendy in Perthshire. His family were Jacobites and as such, he joined Lord Nairn's Battalion as a surgeon during the 1715 rebellion. While serving, he was captured, taken to Newgate Prison in London and sentenced to death. However, thanks to the influence of his friends and scientists, he was given a reprieve at midnight on the night before his execution.

Back home, he continued with scientific practices and published writings on anatomy and surgery. By 1720, Blair was based in Boston, Lincolnshire, where he practised medicine and studied botany. In 1723, he published Volume 1 of the encyclopaedia of botany, *Phamaco-Botanologia* – completing up to the letter H before his death in 1728.

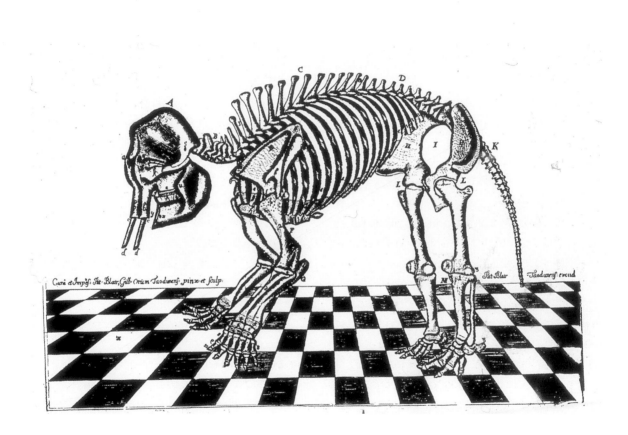

Cura et Imprefs: Pat: Blair, Gilb: Orum Taodunenf: pinx: et sculp: Pat: Blair   Taodunenf: excud

5. The Broughty Ferry Nature Reserve

The Broughty Ferry Nature Reserve starts at the north end of Broughty Ferry Esplanade, just fifteen minutes' drive from Dundee city centre.

Look out for bank voles that live in the long grass and can often be spotted crossing the paths, and keep your eyes peeled for toads, songbirds and tawny owls. If you're lucky you may even see roe deer hiding in the undergrowth.

The reserve also boasts a wide variety of wildflowers including Bluebell, Sea Lyme Grass and Meadow Saxifrage – all best admired in May and June.

Surprisingly, lumps of lava can also be seen throughout the Reserve. This is because the Reserve is an ancient raised beach. During the Ice Age, vast areas of Scotland were pushed into the earth under ice which was, in places, more than one mile thick. The seas inundated land that was previously dry and as the ice melted, new beaches were formed, allowing the land to rise and the River Tay and North Sea to assume their current positions.

This meant that the new sandy beaches were left high and dry and today the sand dunes lie on top of bedrock made up of Andesitic Lava, which was pushed up from underground.

See what treasures you can uncover in the Broughty Ferry Nature Reserve.

6. The Fisherman's Graveyard

Hidden along a small alley leading off Fisher Street, is an old burial ground that is steeped in history and remains one of Broughty Ferry's best-kept secrets.

It was originally the burial ground of a Pre-Reformation chapel which was abandoned around 1670.

The majority of the gravestones date from the late eighteenth century and are numbered from left to right, starting at the south-west corner of the graveyard. Most are upright stones but there are also some table stones and nearly all the stones feature inscriptions.

When the graveyard was in use, very few people could read or write. As such, some of the stones display a variety of easily recognisable symbols rather than words. For example, many of the memorials serve as a reminder of Broughty Ferry's long association with the sea and use symbols such as ships, compasses and anchors.

The small village of Broughty Ferry, four miles to the east of Dundee, began life as a fishing hamlet known as Partan Craig, meaning 'Crab Rock'. The arrival of the railway in the 1830s meant the town became more accessible. Today, this railway station is the oldest working station in Scotland.

The fishing industry peaked in the 1880s and during this time, a cluster of fisherfolks' cottages were built around the harbour and shoreline, many of which still exist today. Take a look at Barometer Cottage on the corner of Fisher Street and Bell's Lane for a glimpse into the area's maritime past. The cottage is so-called because it features a cased barometer on the exterior that was installed in 1859 and whose readings saved the Broughty Ferry fishing fleet from a disaster in 1881. Or look up at the roof of the East Church on Queen Street that boasts fish-scale decoration.

Other symbols that feature on the gravestones in

the burial ground include skulls, crossed bones and an hour-glass that represents the passage of time.

The cherubs or angels that are carved on the top of the stones symbolise either the soul ascending to heaven or the grave of a child. Some stones even list the names of young children who had died – a stark reminder of the high rate of infant mortality that was experienced at the time.

Burials were not restricted to people living in the immediate area. They included farmers, traders and craftsmen from the surrounding villages and even merchants who had been lost at sea or far away from home.

The memorials were made using local sandstone. This was a relatively soft material and over the years, rain and frost have caused the stones to deteriorate. Because of this, many of the inscriptions are now difficult to read and some of the stones have fallen over.

In the south-east corner of the burial ground is the Mort House. This is where coffins used to be kept, usually overnight, before burial because many families didn't have the space to keep them in their own houses.

The graveyard was officially closed in 1867 by order of the Privy Council following a severe outbreak of cholera that claimed twelve lives. Local residents were outraged at the closure and so burials continued in family plots thanks to the efforts of gravedigger William Skirving and undertaker, Matthew Deas. However, Deas and Skirving were convicted of breaking the law. They both pleaded ignorance but were found guilty. Skirving was fined £5 as the main offender and Deas was fined £2. If the fines had not been paid, they would have been sent to prison but the money for Skirving was raised by a public collection in Broughty Ferry. When he returned home, local people carried him through the streets in an armchair!

Visitors can access the burial ground by request at the Ship Inn on Fisher Street, for a returnable deposit of £10.

7. Broughty Ferry Lifeboat Disaster

A lifeboat has been stationed at Broughty Ferry since 1830. However, on 8 December 1959, the station suffered one of the worst lifeboat disasters of the century. An eight-man crew was lost in a storm and the whole town united in grief.

The lifeboat *Mona* had launched in a severe gale at around 3.13am to help the *North Carr Lightship* which had broken away from its main anchor and had started drifting in heavy seas. The *Lightship* did not have any engines so was unable to move without tugs. It was situated at the turning point for ships entering both the Tay and the Forth Estuaries.

The crew on board the *Lightship* eventually managed to stop the drift and were rescued by helicopter but by this time, *Mona* was well on her way to try to help the stranded vessel.

At 4.48am, *Mona* radioed to say she had crossed the bar of the Tay, that the crew had seen the flare from the *Lightship* and that, despite treacherous conditions, they were making progress. After that there was no further contact and the *Mona* was later found stranded on Buddon Sands, near Carnoustie.

Subsequent reports showed that she had capsized in the severe weather and was likely to have first got into difficulties when approaching the bar.

A search party took place the next morning and seven bodies were recovered. The body of the last crew member, George Watson, was never found.

The lifeboat *Mona* rescued 118 people during her twenty-four years of service in Broughty Ferry. Not long after the disaster, she was secretly burned near Edinburgh on confidential orders from Royal National Lifeboat Institution officials in London.

A memorial service was held in St James' Church, the Fisherman's Kirk, at Broughty Ferry and hundreds attended.

Lord Provost William Hughes opened a Broughty Ferry Lifeboat Disaster Fund on the night of the disaster. His staff were unable to keep up with the demand for donations and neighbouring authorities opened their own funds in support. By Saturday, 12 December the fund had reached over £22,000.

Today the *North Carr Lightship* can still be seen, berthed in Dundee's Victoria Dock next to HM Frigate *Unicorn*, the oldest British-built warship still afloat.

8. Dolphin Watching

While visiting Broughty Ferry, you might just be lucky enough to spot a school of bottlenose dolphins.

There are many sightings in the area due to the fact that one of the two populations of bottlenose dolphins in Scotland can be found along the East coast. This is the largest of the two and comprises just fewer than 200 animals.

Another smaller population of around fifty bottlenose dolphins is resident on the West coast of Scotland, around the Hebrides.

The Scottish bottlenose dolphins are the most northerly school in the world and have a tendency to be larger than normal, perhaps as a result of having to bulk up to thrive in the colder northern waters.

The best places in Broughty Ferry to go to look for dolphins are the Esplanade close to Broughty Ferry Castle, the grassy area around the Castle and the breakwater at the Harbour. Or take a visit to the Castle itself and use the lookout point to enjoy a panoramic view of the area, paying close attention to the channel between the Esplanade and Tentsmuir.

The dolphins can usually be seen between May and October and are part of the East-coast population, about half of which spends the summer in the area (the rest being further north in the Moray Firth and off Aberdeen and Montrose). The best time to look for them is from 5 o'clock onwards on summer evenings or when the tide is coming in, as dolphins tend to follow shoals of fish upstream. They also like it when the sea is choppy and when there are no jet-skis or power-boats around.

Other types of dolphin are found in Scotland too, namely the white-beaked dolphin and Risso's dolphin. Even Minke whales visit Scottish waters in the summer! See what you can spot while you're in Broughty Ferry.

9. Baxter Park

Many of Dundee's mills owners made generous efforts to improve conditions both within their mills and throughout the town for the benefit of its citizens.

One such mill owner was linen manufacturer Sir David Baxter. He owned and operated the Dens Works complex. Designed by textile mill engineer Peter Carmichael and constructed in the 1830s and 1840s, Dens Works was one of the biggest and finest mill complexes in the world at the time.

The complex can still be seen today and is described as one of the finest Victorian symbols in Dundee. In 1863, together with his sisters Eleanor and Mary Anne, Sir David Baxter donated Baxter Park to the people of Dundee. The park was opened by the Prime Minister Earl Russell and was marked by a public holiday. Almost 70,000 townspeople attended the ceremony, cheering on a two-mile procession which made its way round Dundee's only formal Victorian park.

Sir David Baxter commissioned Joseph Paxton to design the park. Paxton was viewed as one of the most influential architects and landscape designers of the Victorian age. His works included Crystal Palace in Sydenham and Birkenhead Park in Merseyside, which was the first publically funded park in the world. Baxter Park is the most complete of Paxton's Scottish works.

Over time, as the needs of the public space have changed and thanks to a full historically sensitive restoration plan in the early 1990s, the park has evolved. Today, it boasts bowling greens, tennis courts, modern walkways and a children's play area with the aim of maintaining the space as a vibrant, social and safe area for the community. Meanwhile, the award-winning glass-walled Baxter Park Centre and amphitheatre bring even more life to the park and provide a focal point for community activities and events.

Be sure to look out for the trees in Baxter Park, some of which are recognised as the finest examples of their species in the United Kingdom.

For example, the 'Champion' Cotoneaster is the largest of its kind in Great Britain. There are also Camperdown and Wych Elms, a rare Weeping Oak, and Lime avenues.

Situated in the middle of the main terrace overlooking the south of the park, is the Sandstone Pavilion. It boasts five archways that are supported by Doric columns and an East and West wing. Designed in the Italian loggia style, it was built to protect the ladies of the time from the sun while the gentlemen strolled in the park.

The Pavilion also features an elaborate white marble statue of Sir David Baxter. The statue was built by Sir John Steell, Scotland's leading sculptor at the time. Steell's other great Dundonian work is his statue of Scotland's National Bard, Robert Burns, which is located in Albert Square. Steell viewed this as his best work – despite being well-known for his statue of Sir Walter Scott in the Scott Monument in Edinburgh.

As well as the statue of Sir David Baxter, the Pavilion also boasts a café and a registry office, allowing it to be used for weddings.

In 2007 a mosaic, which was the result of a partnership between the city council and the local community, was installed at the Park Centre, symbolising Baxter's original wish of a park for all.

The People's Park, as it came to be known, was just one of the ways the Baxters went to great lengths to help the citizens of Dundee. They were thought of as good employers because they offered Government contracts which meant they were able to keep their core workforce in times of high unemployment. At Dens Works, Sir David Baxter employed Peter Carmichael as a manager who was innovative in designing both new machinery and new mills.

In many of his designs for new buildings, Carmichael prioritised the improvement of ventilation for the workers and ensured there was always plenty of natural light.

The Baxters also provided a school for their workers' children. They were very interested in education and in 1840 they donated funds to establish the Watt Institute, the precursor to the current University of Abertay, where tradesmen could attend lectures to improve their own education.

Sir David Baxter left £20,000 in his will to establish a technical institute in the city and he also funded the building of the Albert Institute in 1867 (now the McManus Art Gallery and Museum) which was originally built as a reference library. It was recognised at the time as the grandest memorial to Prince Albert outside of London.

Miss Mary Ann Baxter left £130,000 in her will towards a university college which became the present day University of Dundee – one of the many lasting legacies of the family that did so much for the city.

10. Dundee's Grand Canyon

The Dighty Burn is Dundee's underdog river. It is steeped in history and snakes around the back of the city, beginning at the Lundie Burn in the Sidlaw Hills and running from east to west, from Kirkton, through Caird Park, around the north side of Broughty Ferry before reaching the sea somewhere between Broughty Ferry and Monifieth. It stretches fourteen miles in total.

The Burn began several millennia ago and existed long before even the idea of the city of Dundee was a reality. In fact, its history is so significant that the Burn has been described by geology experts as a miniature Grand Canyon.

This is because much of Dundee is built above rock which has come from lava. The lava flowed through the area millions of years ago – the Dundee Law is the plug of an extinct volcano. Today some of this lava is exposed because the Dighty Burn has cut through all the soft rock, revealing the hard lava underneath.

From the sixteenth century, the Dighty Burn was known as Scotland's hardest working stream. It provided power for industry – there were millponds, water channels, drying greens and mill buildings with water wheels all along its banks. During the eighteenth century there were around fifty-six mills on the Burn for grain production and later for the waulking of woollen cloth. Bleachfields – open areas of land where newly manufactured cloth was laid out in the sun to bleach – were also established, some of which remained until the twentieth century.

Today, the Dighty Burn is a popular walking route for many and there are lots of points of interest to look out for along the way. Linlathen East footbridge for example, spans the Burn at the eastern entrance and dates from 1795 to 1810. Or make your way to the Monifieth end of the Burn to see the impressive

Seven Arches viaduct that once carried the traffic of the Dundee and Forfar Direct Railway which opened in 1870.

As might be expected, the Burn is shrouded in woodland and grassy banks. A volunteer project called 'Dighty Connect' works to enhance the green spaces along the Burn through conservation and cultural activities. Projects range from creating amphibian habitats to building mosaic benches and everybody is welcome to get involved. Why not lend a helping hand during your time in the Dundee area while admiring one of its hidden gems?

11. General Monck's Treasure

Legend has it that treasure worth billions of pounds lurks on the seabed somewhere between Broughty Ferry Castle and the south shore of the River Tay from Broughty Ferry, past the Abertay Sands – all just waiting to be discovered!

The cargo is known as General Monck's Loot and dates from 1651 when a fleet of sixty ships that Monck had commandeered, foundered in the Tay in a bad storm.

It is believed that the loot included £200,000 worth of gold coins as well as other precious gold and silver items and religious artefacts, with a total value of £2.5 billion in today's money.

The treasure and coins were originally pillaged from Dundee when Monck's troops sacked the Royalist city in 1651. In 1649, Charles II had written to Dundee's town clerk Alexander Wedderburn from exile in Brussels, to thank him and the citizens of Dundee for their services to the late Charles I. At the time, Dundee was a walled town and was considered to be among the safest towns in Britain, so much so that the city of Edinburgh stored its gold reserves there and the Viscount of Newburgh, as well as the Earls of Tweeddale and Buccleuch, kept their wealth in the town.

However, Dundee's Monarchist stance angered the Republican statesman Oliver Cromwell who had previously overcome Royalist forces. As a result, Cromwell's commander-in-chief in Scotland, General Monck, laid siege to Dundee assisted by his 7,000-strong Puritan army.

Monck's tactics involved recruiting a man that looked like a child who then joined in games with the town's children inside and outside the city walls. By doing this, the spy determined that Dundee's soldiers were usually drunk by lunchtime. Monck used this intelligence to breach the city's northern wall with three days of cannon fire and then waited until lunchtime before he attacked. Moncks' troops gladly carried out his instruction with the promise that they could pillage the town for twenty-four hours if they successfully gained entry.

Dundee's drunken soldiers defended the town for fifteen minutes. Monck's army killed the defenders and Dundee's Governor, Robert Lumsden, displaying his head on a spike for all to see. Monck's army pillaged the town for three days in total during which time up to 500 men, women and children lost their lives.

After the attack, Monck commandeered sixty ships from Dundee harbour to take his plunder to Leith. It was these ships that sank, along with their treasure and those on board. Monck was travelling on one of the biggest ships – which survived.

Over the years, teams of treasure

hunters have undertaken exploratory surveys of the seabed using advanced underwater survey technology. The treasure has never been found, nor have any remains of the many lost ships in the fleet. One team, however, did discover a 9-pound solid-shot cannon ball which is believed to date from the time of Monck's attack and, around thirty years ago, the remains of a sword that also dated to that time, were discovered near the north-easterly point of Tentsmuir Forest in Fife.

Historians have argued for centuries about the fate of the fleet of General Monck. Many believe the vessels would have been quickly covered by the Tay's shifting sands, meaning the treasure could still be buried there today. Or, maybe all the treasure was on Monck's ship and made it to Leith?

Of course, not everyone believes the story of Monck's treasure, instead labelling it as folklore. Some maintain that the story of the shipwreck is based on one vague account which came to light over twenty years after Monck's attack. On top of this, it is thought that the Cromwellian Government records would have kept a detailed account of such a major shipping disaster – none of which exist.

Whatever you believe, who can resist a tale of treasure?

Bibliography

Books

Begg, Hugh M., Davey, Chris & Davey, Nancy. *The Memory of Broughty Ferry*. 2013.

Brotchie, Alan and Herd, Jack. *Wheels Around Dundee*. Ayrshire: Stenlake Publishing Limited, 2002.

Douglas, Gordon. *We'll Send Ye Tae the Mars: The Story of Dundee's Legendary Training Ship*. Edinburgh: Black & White Publishing, 2008.

Fitt, Matthew. *Time Tram Dundee*. New Lanark: Waverley Books, 2006.

Gauldie, Enid. *The Bonnets of Bonnie Dundee*. Invergowrie: Waterside Press, 1993.

King, Brian. *Undiscovered Dundee*. Edinburgh: Black & White Publishing, 2011.

Macintyre, Lorn and Adamson, Peter. *Dundee: Portrait of a City.* St Andrews: Alvie Publications, 2006.

McKean, Charles, Harris, Bob and Whatley, Christopher A. *Dundee: Renaissance to Enlightenment*. Edinburgh: Edinburgh University Press, 2009.

McKean, Charles and Whatley, Patricia. *Lost Dundee*. Edinburgh: Birlinn Ltd, 2013.

Ogilvy, Graham. *Dundee: A Voyage of Discovery*. Edinburgh: Mainstream Publishing Company Ltd, 1999.

Scott, Andrew Murray. *Modern Dundee. Life in the City Since World War Two.* Derby: Breedon Books Publishing Company Limited, 2006.

Springfield, David. *Dundee Reflections. More Than Image*. 2011.

She Feeds the Sea. Writing from the Dighty Burn. Kirriemuir: Salty Press, 2012.

Watson, Norman. *Dundee in Old Picture Postcards*. Netherlands: European Library, 1997.

Whatley, Christopher A. *Victorian Dundee: Image and Realities*. Edinburgh: Edinburgh University Press Ltd, 2011.

Magazines

City of Dundee Scotland A Chronicle of The City's Office Bearers, Chambers, Regalia, Castles and Twin Cities. Dundee City Council Public Relations, 2004.

The Courier Magazine, Liquid Assets, Uncovering the lost wells of Dundee, D.C.Thomson & Co Ltd., 2014

Websites

www.news.bbc.co.uk/1/hi/scotland/tayside_and_central/7651553.stm

www.eveningtelegraph.co.uk/news/local/parts-of-dundee-built-on-top-of-lava-stream-1.114145

www.dundee.stv.tv/articles/297716-the-law-tunnel-major-visitor-attraction-dundee-deirdre-robertson/

www.bbc.co.uk/scotland/sportscotland/asportingnation/article/0031/

www.broughtyferrylifeboat.org/history.html

www.fdca.org.uk/Lifeboat_Mona.html

bfdt.wordpress.com/2009/07/08/fishermans-graveyard/

www.dundee.com/visit-dundee/attractions.html

www.eveningtelegraph.co.uk/news/local/dundee-s-key-role-in-william-wallace-story-1.436499

www.thecourier.co.uk/news/dundee-service-to-remember-second-world-war-maritime-tragedy-1.36131

www.dundeecivictrust.co.uk/articles/hilltown-history.php

www.dundee.ac.uk/general/campusguide/virtualtour/geddes/

www.dundee.ac.uk/botanic/visitorinformation/grounds/citycampus/

canmore.rcahms.gov.uk/en/site/165116/details/dundee+methven+street+camperdown+works+cox+s+stack/

www.buildingsatrisk.org.uk/details/914833

www.scottish-places.info/scotgaz/features/featurefirst90204.html

www.dundeecivictrust.co.uk/articles/dundee-street-names-part-1.php

www.barnhillrockgarden.org.uk/default.htm

www.ninetradesofdundee.co.uk/

www.scottisharchitects.org.uk/architect_full.php?id=100391

www.eveningtelegraph.co.uk/news/local/travelling-in-time-new-book-tracks-history-of-dundee-s-trams-and-buses-1.427228

www.visitscotland.com/info/see-do/camperdown-country-park-p247131

www.walkingstories.com/original/themileystory.htm

news.stv.tv/scotland/123800-memorial-unveiled-to-dundee-submariners/

www.news.stv.tv/tayside/120593-wwii-spycatchers-revealed-after-70-years/

www.visitscotland.com/info/see-do/mills-observatory-p247101

www.dundeecity.gov.uk/supportservs/millsobservatory

bygone.dundeecity.gov.uk/bygone-news/january-1906

www.dundeecity.gov.uk/rangerservice/bfnature

www.princeton.edu/~achaney/tmve/wiki100k/docs/James_Bowman_Lindsay.html

http://www.eurosurf.com/camperdown/house.htm

www.cairdhall.co.uk/organ/

maryslessor.org/mary-slessor/

www.scotlandspeople.gov.uk/Content/Help/index.aspx?r=546&2151

www.dundeemessenger.co.uk/myths-and-legends/the-dundee-dragon

Acknowledgements

Thank you, as ever, to my wonderful husband Kevin for his enduring love, support and patience.
Sincere thanks to all those noted below with whom I worked to help make this book possible. Your guidance and advice has been invaluable.

For more information about the campaign to re-open the Law Tunnel and how to get involved, visit: www.facebook.com/DundeeLawTunnel?fref=ts

Special thanks to:
Alice La Rooy
Ann Lolley
Barclay Low
Billy Smith
Bob Hovell
David Barr
D C MacRae
Deirdre Robertson
Deirdre Sweeney

Dr Andrew Jeffrey
Dr Lawrie Mitchell
Dr Neil Burford
Dr Phillip Hammond
Elizabeth Gillan
Father Clive Clapton
Frank Wielbo
Gordon Douglas
Eileen Moran
Iain Flett

Innes A. Duffus
Jean Forbes
Joe Duffy
Joe Hughes
John Richardson
Kevin McMullan
Laura Cooper
Mary Henderson
Mary Saunders
Matthew Jarron

Nancy Davey
Neil Dobson
Philip Rourke
Professor Chris Whatley
Rhona Rodger
Rod Gordon
Roddy Isles
Susan Gillan

Credit is due to the following people and organisations for kind permission to use their photography:

City Centre – Caird Hall, Dundee

The Finest Concert Organ in the United Kingdom – Caird Hall, Dundee.

The Nine Incorporated Trades – www.ninetradesofdundee.co.uk/

Jack the Ripper in Dundee – Wikimedia.

General Monck's Treasure – Wikimedia.

James Chalmers: Inventor of the Adhesive Postage Stamp – Leisure and Culture Dundee.

Dundee's Trams - Local History Centre, Dundee Central Library

The Royal Arch – Local History Centre, Dundee Central Library

The Mars Training Ship – Local History Centre, Dundee Central Library

William Wallace – Getty Images.

The Town House – Local History Centre, Dundee Central Library

World Record Seaplane Fight – Wikimedia.

The Law Tunnel – Elliot Simpson

Dundee's Unsung War Heroes – Getty Images.

Macro Micro Studio – Paul Kozlowski

Thomas John MacLagan: Pioneer in the Development of Aspirin – courtesy of Tayside Medical History Museum, University of

Dundee Museum Services

Williamina Fleming: Women and Astronomy – Wikimedia.

Geddes Quadrangle – University of Dundee

Frances Wright: The World's First Feminist – Wikimedia.

The D'Arcy Thompson Zoology Museum – University of Dundee Museum Services

James Bowman Lindsay: Let There Be Light! – Wikimedia.

Patrick Blair: The First Doctor in Britain to Dissect an Elephant – courtesy of Tayside Medical History Museum, University of Dundee Museum Services

Dolphin Watching – Mònica Arso, University of St Andrews